SHADOWS' REVOLUTION
Cracking the Content and Breaking the Molds

Releasing thoughts and stories from the
physical medium imprisonment.
Deposing the averages from
their meanings.

ORESTES CARVALHO

I once thought true friendships didn't need to be refreshed with superficial small talks. Once one becomes a true friend this person would be a true friend forever, no matter the time, no matter the distance. Meeting again would be as if we were just continuing an interrupted conversation.

However, in my journey through this book I've learned that even if I was right, I have been missing the point about small-talking among friends. Because a conversation among friends is less about the content of the conversation and more about the pleasure of keeping in touch, participating, making sure we are part of the same net that can keep us up or protect us from our falls.

For my family. For Andrea, William and Luca, source of my day-to-day joy. For Milene whom I keep in my heart, despite living so far away. For my parents Lina and Joel who guided me when I was setting my roots.

For my sisters, Helena, Flavia and Eneida and for my long time friends, including the ones with whom I haven't contacted for so long.

For the valuable feedback they gave me when I was putting this book together, thanks to Paul Bagdon, Gilberto Brunato, Jim Kozlowski, Oswaldo Mello, Herson Manfrinato, Jaime Szulc, Andy Wlson and Art Roberts.

Contents

Connecting the Dots

Think about a couple that has only had a carriage as a means of transport for their entire lives. They never saw a car until we give them one. First thing they do is to attach their horses to pull their new car. Second thing they do is to conclude their old carriage was better.

Like that couple, many of us once said: CDs are better. DVDs are better. Newspapers are better. And nothing can be better than holding and feeling a physical book.

Like that old couple, many of us didn't realize the concept of inert "content" is an old paradigm, which has been engraved in our minds through the last 500 years. Most of us couldn't fully understand yet that "content" is about to leave the main stage, giving room for "contact," services and live debate. Many teenagers already know this, while many adults can't understand it because they keep trying to pull the new ideas using their old horses.

Why did it take so long for music companies to understand the transformation that was happening in their industry? This book shows this transformation is just the beginning. The same kind of change is about to happen with printed books, general printed material and all other modern mediums[1] that store and transport all kinds of information.

---

[1] Throughout the book, instead of media I will use mediums as plural of medium in order to make sure the reader understands I'm talking about the material that holds and transport data and not about the press.

Many people talk about superficial waves. Technological cycles. Clash of generations. Behavioral fads. But most of us didn't realize yet we are in the middle of a subtle but very deep revolution – the deepest one in the last 500 years, since Gutenberg's printing press. Rather than cyclical waves we are facing a tsunami, which is bringing down the literate-mass-media era. We are facing a revolution that is about to change all kinds of businesses and all aspects of our lives. A revolution that is bringing new concepts we can't even articulate well, as they don't fit in our old paradigms.

How can we understand a car and its implications if all we know are carriages and horses? How can we understand music if we are deaf? We need a way to anchor new concepts to our old knowledge. We need a way to translate new concepts into a language we understand. We need a metaphor.

This book brings the metaphors that will help you do such translation, drawing a cohesive picture of what is going on at the beginning of this twenty-first century. Once you connect the waves and recognize the tsunami, you will be in a better position to ride it, leveraging its power. The others who can't see beyond loosely connected waves and trends will remain being caught by surprise.

This book is intended to be thought provoking and a conversation starter around this subtle revolution and its implications for our businesses and our lives. It brings many intriguing and counterintuitive insights that will make you rethink the way you communicate with your customers and friends, the way you advertise, the way you define your competition, the way you research and create your products and services, the way you sell and distribute them.

It will help you understand the new generations, born and raised in the digital world. It will help you understand what has happened with the music industry and what is about to happen with all other media and communication industries.

The title "Shadows' Revolution" is a metaphor playing with the idea of Plato's shadows (see the prologue). It relates "content" to locked shadows – just inert representations of real life events. In the literate-mass-media era these contents, or shadows, are massively traded in a one-way distribution channel. The **"shadows' revolution"** concerns the event of releasing the inert and locked content from the imprisonment imposed by the physical medium, giving it back the freedom of the old village days, throwing it back into a collaborative, ever-changing, living stream.

And as we move back to participative conversations through multiple-way channels, every individual recovers his or her identity. Each individual contributes with a different piece to construct the whole. The old homogenous and passive audience, from the old literate-mass-media society, fades away, causing the symbolic death of the "average-consumer," because the passive average-consumer has no place in the emerging society – the hyper-oral society.

...

Rather than an authoritative and inert statement – as it was supposed to be in the old literate-mass-media world – this book intends to be an interactive live debate. So please, be active, connect to the book's website [2] and place your comments, participate in the discussions, challenge the ideas, suggest changes, read other people comments. I will change the body of the pages as we learn from each other. You won't learn from me but from a live multiple-way conversation. It is time to abandon the passive consumption and to jump into the debate. Place your comments. Help us – the other readers and me – to construct the whole.

For each chapter of this book you will find a page in the book's website.

You will see my creative contribution to this book is primarily connecting dots as the book weaves many different insights from many visionary people. You will see many excerpts and references with links to their respective articles and sites. (I expect you go after many of those links so you can build your own journey.) Linearity and passivity are part of the old paradigms that are about to die. I hope you actively participate so we build this together, more like a new-era live conversation rather than an inert book of the old era.

---

[2] Go to www.ShadowsRevolution.com

What you will find in each chapter:

Preface – Writing a Book about the End of Books: the original reasons that triggered the development of the book and the website.

Prologue – A Tale about Shadows: a symbolic summary of the whole book. It plays with the underlying analogy that gave title to this work.

Chapter One – Unnoticed Revolutions: a discussion about the difficulty of recognizing deep revolutions when we are in the middle of them.

Chapter Two – Changing Media, Changing Us: a discussion about how the dominance of the print medium has transformed our civilization.

Chapter Three – Back to the Village: a discussion about how the digital medium is transforming us again, somehow bringing back elements of the pre-literate culture, moving us to a hyper-oral society.

Appendix to Chapter Three – Wikis, Participative bottom-up creation vs. Top-down authoritative design: a discussion about wikis as a remarkable expression of the hyper-oral society.

Chapter Four – The Print Mold and the Mass Media Era: a discussion about how the print medium led the way for the mold concept and for mass production, increasing our society productivity and wealth, erecting business empires.

Chapter Five – Landgrab Fight in the Old Media's Land: a discussion about how the digital medium is breaking down silos, changing the nature of the competition and reshaping the business landscape.

Chapter Six – The Crumbling Advertising Mold: a discussion about how the traditional, one-way, cluttered advertising model is giving way to a two-way, pulled (and therefore more precise and less intrusive) model.

Chapter Seven – A Scale-free World, for Good or for Bad?: a discussion about how the mold concept, and the related average-thinking, increased productivity but imposed uniformity and killed individuality. It shows that now we are moving to a scale-free world released from molds and averages, presenting alternative perspectives and implications to our future.

Chapter Eight – Mapping the Media Pipelines: a parallel between water and content, between water pipelines and media pipelines. A map showing all media pipelines getting into our homes with related devices.

Chapter Nine – The Hypermedium: a discussion about how the new digital pipeline is becoming the dominant medium of a new era, radically changing the information supply chain.

Chapter Ten – The Digital Shelf: a discussion about the autocracy of the physical shelf and about the digital medium role on the democratization of the offering, of the distribution and of the production of information goods, leading to a world of abundant choice.

Chapter Eleven – Paradox of Choice?: Alternative perspectives on the issue of abundant choice – is it good or bad? – and implications to internet sites, search engines, aggregation models, filtering, recommendation and people participation.

Epilogue – The Breathing Mesh: this chapter closes the loop, putting in contrast the old literate-mass-media paradigm and the new hyper-oral-society paradigm, showing top-down-hierarchical-intelligent-design approach is giving way to bottom-up-sprouting-order and a new kind of life is emerging from the mesh.

SHADOWS' REVOLUTION
Cracking the Content and Breaking the Molds

Releasing thoughts and stories from the
physical medium imprisonment.
Deposing the averages from
their meanings.

Figure 1: Image from a banner for the peace movement
in Australia in the 1950s

Writing a Book about the End of Books

In the preface we look at the original reasons that triggered the building of this book and of the website. We talk about the realization that the explosion of texting and the decline of interest in books among teenagers are not fads, and are not bad. They are merely like symptoms of a new way of thinking and a new way of communicating.

"We don't read whole books anymore."

On the positive side, Gen M students tend to be extraordinarily good at finding and manipulating information. And presumably because modern childhood tilts toward visual rather than print media, they are especially skilled at analyzing visual data and images, observes Claudia Koonz, professor of history at Duke University. A growing number of college professors are using film, audio clips and PowerPoint presentations to play to their students' strengths and capture their evanescent attention. It's a powerful way to teach history, says Koonz. "I love bringing media into the classroom, to be able to go to the website for Edward R. Murrow and hear his voice as he walked with the liberators of Buchenwald."

Another adjustment to teaching Generation M: professors are assigning fewer full-length books and more excerpts and articles. (Koonz, however, was stunned when a student matter-of-factly informed her, "We don't read whole books anymore," after Koonz had assigned a 350-page volume. "And this is Duke!" she says.

See **The Multitasking Generation** by Claudia Wallis, Mar'06, at Time U.S. website. (Wallis, 2006)

Current teenagers are peculiar: shorter attention span, shorter texts, fewer books,[3] more instant messaging and SMS.

Some of these conceptual changes are hard to understand. What is the point of SMS? Why go through the pain of typing truncated messages with your big thumbs in your small cell phone, scrolling through letters until you find the one you need, when you could just press a few numbers and make a call? What about instant messaging? Why this new generation loves to keep so many simultaneous online messages?

Searching for answers, I've "googled" the question: "What is the point of instant messaging?" These were some of the answers I've found:[4]

"Because then like if you don't want someone to hear you talking then text is silent."

---

[3] Take a look at "Twilight of the Books" by Caleb Crain, Dec'07, at The New Yorker. (Crain, 2007)

[4] See "What is the point of instant messaging" at Yahoo answers. (Yahoo_Answers, 2008)

"And if someone is busy or something and say they can't talk then you just send them in a message what you want to say."

"Sometimes you do not want to call someone just say one thing or just remind someone of something…"

"because texts are cheaper than calls…"

"…you can do a lot of other things while texting…"

"Plus then if you are talking about a touchy situation and you do not want to like tell the person the truth or something then you have time to think of what you are going to say."

These could be good reasons if we assume the messages carry valuable content. However most of the messages I've seen are similar to the one quoted by Claudia Wallis in her Multitasking Generation article:[5]

"…Several IM windows are also open, revealing such penetrating conversations as this one with a MySpace pal:

MySpacer: suuuuuup!! !(Translation: What's up?)

Piers: wat up dude

MySpacer: nmu (Not much. You?)Piers: same"

Is this a teenager thing? Will teenagers change once they grow up and get a job? I remember when I committed myself to not wasting my time nor my friends' time sending emails without a clear purpose. Is there any reason for this new generation to keep sending those empty messages? The

---

[5] See "The Multitasking Generation" by Claudia Wallis, Mar'07, at Time Magazine web site. (Wallis, 2006)

time of well written letters is gone. Don't modern-day young people care about the content?

Maybe not. In fact, I've been learning lack of content can be one of the reasons they prefer instant messaging: "...*well you not just going to call someone and say hey whats up for them to say nothing and them hang up...*" wrote someone when answering to the question – "what is the point of text messaging?"

OK. So, maybe, when instant messaging, people don't care much about what is written but about keeping in touch. Maybe it is just a way to say you are there, just an electronic handshake.

Such insight triggered a strong shift in my line of thought. Suddenly I realized I had been stuck in an old paradigm where the world of writing and the world of talking weren't supposed to mix with each other. In that old paradigm, writing was supposed to carry well thought out content. We were supposed to organize and package our ideas, giving them a logical flow before sending them to anyone.

> **It's not about the content but about the contact.**

I dug further into such insight and I found that teens don't think of their emails, and instant messages as writing. "*... exchanging emails, instant messages, texts, and social network posts is communication that carries the same weight to teens as phone calls and between-class hallway greetings. ...they do not believe that communication over the internet or text messaging is writing...*" [6]

---

[6] See the research "Writing, Technology and Teens," Pew Internet, 2008 at pewinternet.org (Lenhart, Arafeh, Aaron, & Macgill, 2008)

I've learned it is not about the content but about the contact.

I've learned people of new generations are building a much larger social network. While people from older generations used to have just a few friends with whom they would play and talk – through the phone or in a face-to-face gathering – current teenagers keep up with many more friends.

But having so many friends, how do they prevent social distance to grow?

They do it by keeping a constant flow of contacts, through SMSs and instant messages – like multiple blips to different people in different groups at the same time. It is a different model. Less contact, with many more people, demanding a constant flow of contact, lots of little contacts, just a blip on the screen, just a way of "checking in."[7]

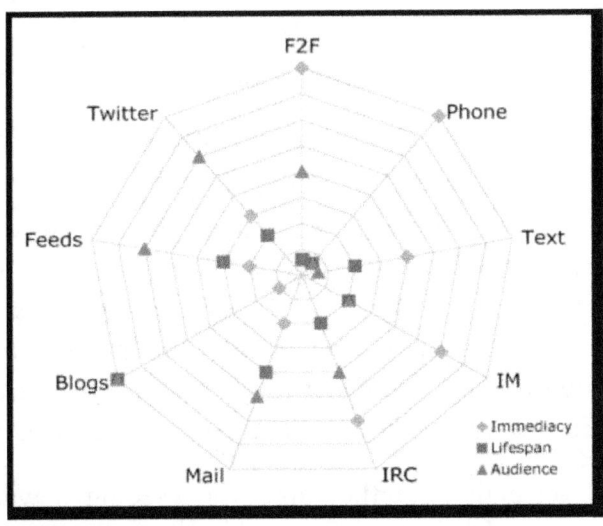

Figure 2: On Communication (Bray, 2007)

---

[7] Grant McCracken coined the term "pinging the hive" a few years ago when he farsightedly identified this change on the way people were communicating and managing their relationships. See his blog at www.cultureby.com

It works like a radar screen, or a sonar screen, where people are constantly "pinging" each other, keeping the links in the network active and the information flowing within their screen.

> The "ping" word started to be used in a network environment as the name of a protocol that sends a message to another computer and awaits acknowledgment. It is often used to check if another computer in the network is reachable.
>
> It is getting a broader meaning as it is becoming part of our everyday language.
>
> "Ping me" does not mean "try to reach my network host to see if it is working." Keith Ferrazzi uses "pinging" to mean keeping in frequent touch with your contacts, to remind them who you are and how helpful you can be to them.
>
> See "Pingg and the evolution of language" (Prange, 2008)

One father was considering the efforts he was planning to accomplish, trying to get closer to his daughter [8]: "*I wonder if I were to text to her? To me texting seems like a waste of time. I prefer to communicate in person, but she's really into texting. Maybe if I talk to her in the way she likes to communicate, I can shrink the wedge between us.*"

I once thought the same way, seeing a waste of time in those empty-of-content messages. But I've learned these truncated messages are key elements in a very effective social radar, keeping track of key information in a large network and at the same time keeping the links of this network alive. It is in fact a very wise strategy to save time.

---

[8] See "Finding common ground with your kids" by Sheri Fisher at Vail Daily 26th Jul'08. (Fisher, 2008)

Just do the math. A teenager generally keeps a few instant messaging windows open at the same time, having a few online buddies in each one of them This way they can keep in touch at once with many of the average 78 "buddies" they have.[9] How could we ever be able to keep refreshing so many relations and how could we ever be able to follow the information flow through this large network of friends if we had to rely on time-consuming phone calls or personal conversations?

Guy Kawasaki was moderating a panel[10] of young adults when he learned this generation could send as many as 4,000 text messages in one month. More than 100 per day! He had a hard time understanding this, the same way I had, before learning these messages have nothing to do with our old "written-word world." They are just blips in these young adults' radar screen. As Mark Frazier points out[11] in his comments on Kawasaki's panel:

> The thing the moderator seems to miss is these kids #1 concern is managing their time and attention. These kids use SMS text messaging because they can politely do it any time and any place. It doesn't demand attention from the recipient. This is the same reason they use MySpace and Facebook. They don't have time to personally deal with all their social interactions. The moderator incorrectly assumed these kids are missing

---

[9] See "Teen Technology All About Friendships" referring to a Survey with 18,000 teenagers done in 2007 by MTV and Nickelodeon in association with Microsoft Digital Advertising Solutions.(MTV, 2007)

[10] See "Is Advertising Dead ?" by Guy Kawasaki, Sep'06 at blog.guykawasaki.com. (Kawasaki, 2006)

[11] See "Information Generation" by Mark Frazier, Jan'07 at markproffitt.com (Frazier, 2007)

social interaction because much of it is not done face to face.

This is the exact opposite of the truth. These kids are managing hyper social behavior. They use technology to stay connected with friends and make connections with possible new friends.[12]

. . .

Once I made such a paradigm shift, a new world opened up in front of me. New ideas and discoveries proliferated. I became so thrilled that I thought I could write a very interesting book about them. But as I worked on the book, I realized I was still locked in my old world paradigms. Ironically I was writing a book about how people were losing their interest in the old-style books, about how the old one-way expositions were being replaced by participation and multiple-ways conversations. As I thought more about this contradiction I realized I wanted to do more things than a standard book would allow me to do.

I wanted to discuss the ideas. I wanted my original thoughts to evolve incorporating all the feedback I could get, becoming more robust after each reader comment. I didn't want the ideas to be inert on a piece of paper. I wanted them alive; I wanted debate and evolution.

I wanted the readers to be able to build their journey themselves while diving through these insights, defining themselves how deep they would like to go, which of my

---

[12] Guy Kawasaki has learned it. Currently he is sending hundreds of messages himself and has become the most followed person in Twitter. See "By the number: The Most Influential Twitterers" by Andy Greenberg, Jan'09 at Forbes.com (Greenberg, 2009)

sources they would like to read, which readers' comments or forums were worth their time.

So, I've shaken off my old paradigms and I've started working on a website. I've kept a printed version for the people – like me – who think the display technology is not good enough, yet, to displace printed paper. Beyond this printed version, I've built a website that, like a traditional book, carries the book structure – prologue, chapters, etc. However, unlike a book, the website is not supposed to have the one-way-I-write-you-read pretense of truth and the feeling of closure of traditional books. This website is intended to be an open, unfinished debate. It will change every time a comment is added to any chapter or forum, and I will keep the body of the chapters alive, changing them, as I learn from you, through our online discussions.

While in a printed book author and readers are apart, we will build the website together. Instead of my-ideas, one-way, author-to-many old style flow, we will build our-ideas, multiple-ways, many-to-many new age flow. Rather than a hierarchy we will build a mesh.

Rather than a linear reading, like most books presume, you will surf through the website, jumping around, from hyperlink to hyperlink. And I hope you get as excited, surfing through these thoughts, as I did.

I hope you engage with us (the other readers and me) in a stimulating debate, enriching our journey.

I hope you have fun.

A Tale about Shadows

This is a symbolic summary of the whole book. It plays with the underlying analogy that gave the title to this work.

Plato's Shadows [13]

The Allegory of the cave

Imagine prisoners who have been held their entire lives looking at shadows projected on a cave wall. They can't move. They can't turn their heads. The only things they see are the shadows.

These prisoners would mistake appearance for reality. They would think the things they see on the wall (the shadows) are real; they would know nothing of the real causes of the shadows.

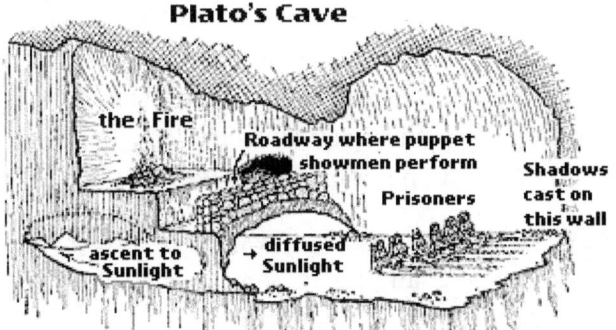

Plato's Cave

Figure 3: From (Great Dialogues of Plato: Complete Texts of the Republic, Apology, Crito Phaido, Ion, and Meno, vol.1, 1999) at (Cohen, 2006)

---

[13] See "The Allegory of the cave" at University of Washington website (Cohen, 2006)

Plato used the shadows analogy to describe how people could mistake appearance for reality. I'm hitchhiking on Plato's shadows idea. I'm using the shadows analogy to help me illustrate:

- how real world events were one day boxed and transformed into content;[14]
- how this fact deeply influenced human social structures and way of thinking;
- how the new paradigm got so rooted in our thinking so we often mistake appearance for reality;
- how digital technology is releasing boxed content transforming it back into real world events;
- how this is deeply influencing, again, people way of thinking.

This is a tale about the end of an era when people used to lock up shadows and massively sell them inside boxes.

Shadows have been around on earth as long as the sunlight. They are light's creations, their live verses, always changing. They were already on earth when humankind appeared and they gladly joined the people, dancing with them around their fires. They would flee to people's dreams at night and come back the next day, participating on the making of human's journey on earth.

They were elusive, not easy to grasp or figure out, continuously changing their shapes. But they were loyal – following their architect dutifully.

---

[14] By "boxing events transforming them into content," I mean attaching the spoken word, the thought, or the singer performance to a physical medium – a piece of paper, a vinyl disc, a magnetic tape, a CD or a DVD. The physical medium is the box. The captured event becomes the content locked up inside the box.

One day someone invented a trap to capture the shadows. So they would never leave. One would be able to collect them. One would be able to possess many shadows. No need to start all over again every morning. And having many shadows would give one a huge power – like having the souls of many people.

Wise men advised against it. Collecting shadows would give the impression of knowledge without the truth, the impression of knowing much but knowing nothing.

But nothing could stop the shadows' trade from grow. It had a shy start. But at some moment the traffic gained momentum, accelerating up to a point when almost everyone was participating in a massive trade of shadows. Shadows were being captured, boxed and sold by billions.

And while the trade expanded, the world was totally reshaped.

At first were the humans imprisoning the shadows; but then humankind became addicted and totally dependent on them. And people couldn't differentiate anymore the shadows from the light. People started taking for real what used to be just a shadow dancing around the fire. The enlightening dancing experience had given place to a deceiving physical private possession. An evanescent event had become content inside a box. And boxes of content laid inert, scattered all over the place.

• • •

People once used to drink at the stream. It was a live experience filled by smell, sounds and feelings of all nature, and feedback of all those people around. One day people learned how to have water delivered to their houses in buckets; and after that, through pipes. This brought them great comfort but once they got used to consume what was prepared and delivered to them, they forgot how was to be at the source, how was to participate instead of just consume at the predefined end.

. . .

Like water in buckets, shadows were trapped in pre-formatted content and scattered all over the place. People loved to play with them but the shadows couldn't hear. The shadows couldn't debate. They would only repeat the one-way sequence recorded before they got packed. The live appearance was deceptive. In fact, they were inert and insulated within their boxes. They were like stagnant water ponds far away from the main stream.

Until the day someone found out a way to connect those ponds, building a mesh of ponds. Until the day someone opened the dams allowing free multiple-way flows among the mesh of scattered ponds.

That day, a subtle but powerful transformation started to happen – that mesh started to breathe. It became alive. Then, the live event broke out of the frozen content shell, releasing all those locked shadows. And the people were thrown back into the stream – from which they had been kept apart for so long. Passive consumption gave way to collaborative creation. One-way I-talk-you-listen lectures gave way to multiple-way rich conversations. I-tell-you-the-facts-you-just-listen (or read) authorial authority of closed pretense truths gave way to live debates and ever changing collective interpretations. People were, once again, living the show, not just watching the shadows projected on the wall. They were drinking at the stream directly connected to the whole, living the moment, together, within the breathing mesh.

ONE

Unnoticed Revolutions

> In this chapter we talk about the difficulty of recognizing deep revolutions when we are in the middle of them. Superficial revolutions are more violent and obvious, but the deeper ones are subtle. They bring new concepts that we can't even articulate as they don't fit in our old paradigms. In this chapter we look at a few changes of youth behavior and ask: are these changes just part of regular tides or is there something deeper going on? We consider a broader look at history can lead us to find the rhymes – meaning metaphors, or similar concepts – that can eventually help us understand what is going on.

Albert Einstein once said: *"You cannot solve a problem in the same frame of mind in which you created it."* In other words: **It is very hard to see the fire when we are inside the pot.**[15]

Figure 4: boiling frog

If you drop a few executives in a pot of boiling water, they will, of course, frantically try to clamber out. But if you place them gently in a pot of tepid water and turn the heat on low, they will float there quite placidly...

---

[15] Image from www.housepricecrash.co.uk

> As the water gradually heats up, the executives will sink into a tranquil stupor, exactly like one of us in a hot bath, and before long, with a smile on their faces, they will unresistingly allow themselves to be boiled to death.
>
> Adapted from "The Boiling Frog" at davidsheen.com (Sheen)

The original recipe had a frog in it, instead of executives, but I couldn't stand to hear it anymore. How could someone be so cruel with frogs, even in a figurative way? So I decided to put the frogs out of the pot and go straight to the point: not all revolutions are bloody, noisy and evident; some revolutions can take place relatively unnoticed. *"The reason has often been given that the most profound revolutions are not those that overturn institutions, but those that leave institutions standing while emptying them of all significance."* [16]

Trying to put frogs in pots probably wouldn't work anyway as stated by Professor Doug Melton from Harvard University Biology Department:[17] *"If you put a frog in boiling water, it won't jump out. It will die. If you put it in cold water, it will jump before it gets hot - they don't sit still for you."* Of course, this is also true to many executives. Many of them wouldn't sit still. They would probably jump out – using a golden parachute if they have one – leaving behind their organizations boiling with the water...

---

[16] See "CAMPAIGN 2000 III: Our Inglorious Revolution - race and culture" by John O'Sullivan, Apr'00 at findarticles.com (O'Sullivan, 2000)

[17] See "Next Time, What Say We Boil a Consultant" by Fast Company, Oct'95 at fastcompany.com (Fast_Company, 2007)

But how can someone – or an organization – know if it has come the time to jump out of the pot?

The answer seems to be easy when we look things in retrospect. However, wise people have been missing many and many times the signs of major changes. Even great minds have failed to feel the heat every now and then:

- Winston Churchil, British Prime Minister said in 1939: *"Atomic energy might be as good as our present day explosives, but it is unlikely to produce anything more dangerous."*

- Thomas Edison in 1880s: *"The phonograph has no commercial value at all."*

- Charlie Chaplin in 1916: *"The cinema is little more than a fad. It is canned drama. What audiences really want to see is flesh and blood on the stage."*

All of them misread the signs and couldn't perceive the fire heating their pot.[18]

Now, what if I tell you our civilization is about to boil, as it has never done before? Have you noticed the fire? (I'm not talking about Global Warming, nor the Economic Crisis...)

Some will say there is no fire: *"What force will shake our world and take it forward in the twenty-first century? There is no sign of any social revolutions as yet, unless one counts the 'green revolution' that in some ways seems to want to turn the clock back. We shall have to see."*[19]

---

[18] See "Top 87 Bad Predictions about the Future," May'07 at 2spare.com (2Spare, 2006)

[19] See "Ten days that shook the world. The Russian Revolution revisited," by Mick Hume at spiked-online.com (Hume, 2007)

To many of us it seems we will never see again anything like the French Revolution, Russian Revolution or the Civil Rights Movement. The most we can see ahead is the natural and peaceful expansion of the Green Movement started in the 80s. After the socialist parties, we had the green parties, and that's it. It seems the prospect of deep social revolutions has been knocked down, together with the Berlin Wall.

On the other hand, we have the ones who say they already see bubbles in the water: *"The last 25 years in technology have just been the warm-up act. Now we are going into the main event... an era in which technology will truly transform every aspect of business, of government, of society, of life."*[20]

Yes, maybe we can agree there is some heat. But how can we know if what is coming is not just another wave within the already familiar technology life cycle?   Aren't these changes more technical rather than social?

We can try to find out by looking at the behavior of people. We can look at the people who will define the future. We can look at the young people, the generation Y.

This new generation has a challenging behavior on dealing with authorities:

> GENERATION Y's disdain for authority has been blamed for an alarming increase in assaults on police.
>
> It's a Badge of Honor, Courier Mail, Australia, Jan. 28th, 2008, page 3 (Swanwick, 2008)

---

[20] Carly Fiorina, former HP CEO, quoted in "It's a Flat World, After All" by Thomas Friedman, Apr'05 at nytimes.com (Friedman, 2005)

Generation Y is much less likely to respond to the traditional command-and-control type of management still popular in much of today's workforce... They've grown up questioning their parents, and now they're questioning their employers. They don't know how to shut up, which is great, but that's aggravating to the 50-year-old manager who says, 'Do it and do it now.'... a recent example is a young woman who just started a job at a cereal company. She showed up the first day with a recipe for a new cereal she'd invented.

See "Gen Y: They have arrived at work with a new attitude"
(Armour, 2005)

They don't read whole books anymore:

Claudia Koonz was stunned when a student matter-of-factly informed her, 'We don't read whole books anymore,' after Koonz had assigned a 350-page volume. 'And this is Duke!' she says...

See "The Multitasking Generation" (Wallis, 2006)

They seem to be smarter but more superficial

On the positive side, [Gen Y] students tend to be extraordinarily good at finding and manipulating information. And presumably because modern childhood tilts toward visual rather than print media, they are especially skilled at analyzing visual data and images.

See "The Multitasking Generation" (Wallis, 2006)

They do their homework while listening to their music, talking in their mobile phone and simultaneously holding multiple online conversations.

They seem to be more engaged in community activities and less into reading or into intellectual and spiritual activities. They seem to be more pragmatic.

Of course generation Y is different from their parents' generation, as in all generations. But this difference seems to be more related to how they deal with the new technologies than to radically different social aspirations.

> Every generation of adults sees new technology--and the social changes it stirs--as a threat to the rightful order of things: Plato warned (correctly) that reading would be the downfall of oral tradition and memory. And every generation of teenagers embraces the freedoms and possibilities wrought by technology in ways that shock the elders: just think about what the automobile did for dating.
>
> See "The Multitasking Generation" (Wallis, 2006)

Could those new generation behaviors be signs of upcoming social revolutions?

Again we can feel some heat. But how can we know if this is not just another clash of generations?

Albert Einstein once said: "*You cannot solve a problem in the same frame of mind in which you created it.*" In other words: It is very hard to see the fire when we are inside the pot.

So, we need to broaden our point of view. We need to look for signs, out of the pan, that we can recognize.

Mark Twain once said: "*History doesn't repeat itself but it often rhymes.*"

So, let's search for rhymes. Ultimately we learn through rhymes. Only events that rhyme have meaning. If I tell you " δημοκράτια ", you will probably not understand me. You haven't heard nothing like that before. No resonance in your brain – no meaning. But if I tell you, δημοκράτια means democracy? Now it resonates. But the tune it plays for you will be very different from those tunes played to people from different countries with different political history. We learn as our brain searches for rhymes – in our own experience or in other's stories, so we can translate new ideas to a language we understand.

So what better rhymes with this heat we have been feeling? How can we tell what is coming? Is it just an unusual tide or is it a tsunami? Is it just another technology lifecycle? Is it just another clash of generations?

Ultimately: **Is it time to jump out of the pot, or is this heat just another summer**?

. . .

The Digital Natives, Digital Immigrants

...today's students think and process information fundamentally differently from their predecessors. These differences go far further and deeper than most educators suspect or realize. "Different kinds of experiences lead to different brain structures," says Dr. Bruce D. Perry of Baylor College of Medicine. ...it is very likely that our students' brains have physically changed – and are different from ours – as a result of how they grew up...

Our students today are all "native speakers" of the digital language of computers, video games and the Internet... Those of us who were not born into the digital world but have, at some later point in our lives, become fascinated by and adopted many or most aspects of the new technology are, and always will be compared to them, Digital Immigrants.

Digital Natives are used to receiving information really fast. They like to parallel process and multi-task. They prefer their graphics before their text rather than the opposite. They prefer random access (like hypertext). They function best when networked. They thrive on instant gratification and frequent rewards. They prefer games to "serious" work.

...Digital Immigrants typically have very little appreciation for these new skills that the Natives have acquired and perfected through years of interaction and practice. These skills are almost totally foreign to the Immigrants, who themselves learned – and so choose to teach – slowly, step-by-step, one thing at a time, individually, and above all, seriously.

Excerpts from the paper: "Digital Natives, Digital Immigrants" by Marc Prensky, Oct'01 at marcprensky.com (Prensky, 2001)

Culture Affects The Way We Use Our Brain

Researchers at MIT showed that people from different cultures present different patterns of brain activation when performing similar tasks.

They asked people from USA and East Asia to make some relative and absolute judgments while scanning their brains through magnetic resonance.

They found out Americans, when making relative judgments, activated brain regions involved in attention-demanding mental tasks. Relative judgments are typically harder for Americans because they come from a culture, which values the individual and emphasizes the independence of objects from their contexts. Americans showed much less activation of these regions when making the more culturally familiar absolute judgments.

East Asians showed the opposite tendency, engaging the brain's attention system more for absolute judgments than for relative judgments, which are easier for them as their societies emphasize the collective and the contextual interdependence of objects.

Adapted from Rick Nauert's article at PsychCentral.
(Nauert, 2008)

TWO

Changing Media, Changing Us

In this chapter we bring together parts of outstanding work done by some visionary people about how deeply the dominant medium of a particular time can affect our societies. We talk about how the dominance of print, sparked by Gutenberg, has transformed our society from oral to literate. This will help us understand the transformative potential of the digital medium.

"The medium is the message [21]

Missionaries worked for 25 years with the Tiv tribe in Central Nigeria and saw only 25 baptized believers as a result. Their medium of communication was preaching, which they had learned in Bible school was the way to evangelize. A few years ago some young Tiv Christians set the Gospel story to musical chants, the native medium of communication. Almost immediately the Gospel began to spread like wildfire, and soon a quarter-million Tiv were worshipping Jesus. The Tiv were not as resistant as the missionaries thought. A change in method brought abundant fruit.

See "Faith comes by Hearing? About Oral Societies" by Graydon Colville at globalrecordings.net (Colville)

---

[21] Marshal McLuhan

What is a tree?

Students of Prof. Dino Felluga at Purdue University: *"...
plant with bark, branches and leaves... categorized by
conifer and deciduous kinds. Photosynthesis and
oxygenation were mentioned as important aspects of a
tree's life cycle, and then different uses for trees were
mentioned (paper, construction, shade, etc.). The class
unanimously agreed with this definition."*

Non-literate people in Yugoslavia: *"Surprisingly, there too,
the response to the question was, for the most part,
unanimous and yet completely different: - a tree is like a
man whose arms reach up to heaven but whose roots are
caught in hell."*

What happens is that in the literate world we look to our
written sources. They structure our *"experience of the world
through the conventions of science and taxonomy."* But the
way oral societies think about the world is fundamentally
different, because they have no structured written sources to
recall their experiences. They rely on oral stories that are
recounted and transformed through generations.

*"One way to understand the transformative but largely
unnoticed changes effected by new technologies is to think
about the way that the printed word changed our way of
thinking about the world. That can then help students to
start thinking about the ways postmodern technologies (like
the computer, the television, film, and mechanical image
production) might be subtly but fundamentally changing
our way of thinking about the world around us,"* says Prof.
Dino Felluga. [22]

---

[22] See Prof.Dino Felluga website: <u>General Introduction to the
Postmodern</u> (Felluga, 2003)

There was an age when very few written texts existed and "writing technology" had a hard time to establish itself.

> **❝❝Writing was an attempt to turn living thoughts dwelling in the human mind into mere objects in the physical world.**

Writing was somewhat out of synch with thought. It was slow. It had limited scope – writing could reach just one person at a time while speaking out loud could reach multitudes.

Writing also put people apart as it presupposed distance in time and space between author and reader. Writing disengaged people from direct, interpersonal discussion. It was a solitary task and it was an inert one. A text couldn't debate with someone.[23]

In the ancient Greece, Plato expressed concerns – through Socrates' character in his book, Phaedrus – about the danger of "writing technology." It would lead people to rely on what is written rather than what they were able to think. Writing would destroy memory and would weaken the mind. Writing is inhuman and unresponsive. *"If you ask a text, you get back nothing except the same, often stupid, words... The written word cannot defend itself as the spoken word can; real speech and thought always exist essentially in a context of give-and-take between real persons. Writing is passive, out of it, in an unreal, unnatural world."*[24]

---

[23] Previous three paragraphs adapted from "Post-Gutenberg Galaxy: The Fourth Revolution in the Means of Production of Knowledge." by Stevan Harnard (Harnad, 1991)

[24] See chapter 4 (page 79) of the book "Orality and Literacy: The Technologizing of the World" by Walter J. Ong (Ong, 1988)

"Writing technology" would allow people to read about many things but they would learn nothing; they would have the show of wisdom without the reality.[25] *"Writing was an attempt to turn living thoughts dwelling in the human mind into mere objects in the physical world."* [26]

But the benefits of "writing technology" outdo all possible shortcomings. Writing increases dramatically the human capability to store and recall thoughts and stories. Its adoption was inexorable. So people started to capture living thoughts and to trade them as content inside boxes.

However, it took long time until such trade could significantly reach general people. Oral cultures maintained their oral hegemony long after "writing technology" was invented. For long time just a few members of society were skilled on the art of scribing. And even these scribers wrote in an "oral way." Books were supposed to be recited out loud to a group of people around the reader. "Legere," the latin word for "to read," means read aloud. It requires a qualifier in order to mean read without sound: "legere cum silencio." [27]

Things changed in the fifteenth century, when Gutenberg invented the press with moving types, sealing the end of the Middle Ages and fueling the Renaissance. The printing press changed dramatically and radically the economics of producing books. Before that, books were treated as

---

[25] See also on "Is Writing the Highest Form of Speech?" by Jeff Jarvis. (Jarvis, 2006)

[26] This phrase comes from Wikipedia's "Orality" entry. (Orality, 2009)

[27] See "The life and scholarship of Walter J. Ong," (Saint Louis University, 2008)

treasuries, carried from generations, the first things saved from fires.

> In 1455, Gutenberg demonstrated the power of the printing press by selling copies of a two-volume Bible (Biblia Sacra) for 300 florins each. This was the equivalent of approximately three years' wages for an average clerk, but it was significantly cheaper than a handwritten Bible that could take a single monk 20 years to transcribe.
>
> See "The History of Visual Communication" (Ayiter, 2008)

By the year 1500, printing presses had spread across Europe, producing a few hundred pages per hour and books at a fraction of the original cost.

> The print press introduced Western civilization to some of its sharpest weapons; among them: linear, rational thinking, the preservation and cataloging of a vast assemblage of knowledge, the establishment of standards, the bold documentation and dissemination of forthright, educated opinions.
>
> See "Trends of Anarchy and Hierarchy" by Amanda Griscom (Griscom, 1996)

Despite the concerns expressed by Plato, the "writing technology," now leveraged by printing, came to fill some serious gaps of oral societies:

- *"It permits people to store ideas and retrieve them as needed across time in a highly efficient and accurate way. The absence of this technology in oral societies limits the development of complex ideas and the institutions that depend on them. Only literary cultures have launched phenomenological analyses, abstract classifications, ordered lists and tables."*[28]

- *"Without writing, if thoughts were not expressed in easily remembered forms and were not constantly repeated, they would be lost."*[29]

- *"If in a purely oral culture, you carefully work out a 200-word statement, how do you get it back after you have uttered it? Exact verbal memorization is unreliable without a text to verify recall."*[30]

Writing technology led oral societies into major transformations not just on how we communicated and preserved ideas but also on our behavior and our way of thinking.

There is plenty of good material available online relating some key changes on mindset and behavior that happened as we moved to the new LITERATE SOCIETIES coming from the old ORAL SOCIETIES. In general those changes are interdependent and overlap each other. I've arbitrarily grouped them – listed below – in a way I believed would be more meaningful to our current discussion. I've used many excerpts from my original sources to illustrate such changes. I suggest you surf through these sources after you read the summary I've presented in the next pages. The main sources are listed at the end of this chapter.

---

[28] Excerpt from Wikipedia's "Orality" entry. (Orality, 2009)
[29] From Art Bingham, "Review of Walter J. Ong's book: Orality and Literacy: The Technologizing of the World" (Bingham)
[30] See "The life and scholarship of Walter J. Ong," (Saint Louis University, 2008)

Summary of changes from Oral to Literate societies:

Oral Societies		Literate Societies
Ever changing thought	vs.	Feeling of Closure
Evanescent Event	vs.	Boxed Content
Collective Creation	vs.	Authorial authority
Group of Listeners	vs.	Lonely Reader
Pragmatic, Empathetic Participation	vs.	Individual Abstraction
Aggregative, Redundant, non-hierarchical thought	vs.	Analytical, Linear and Hierarchical thought
Conservative and Agonistically toned	vs.	Investigative and Conciliatory

Table 1: from Oral to Literate Societies

When LITERATE SOCIETY took the place
of the old ORAL SOCIETY:

FEELING OF CLOSURE took the place
of EVER CHANGING THOUGHT

Literate societies think about a book as a final product of thought – ready to be published. There is a feeling of closure, of final version, of completeness, of finished content that never existed in oral societies when the ideas and stories were alive, when they were continuously transforming every time they were told or discussed and passed through generations.

"Print encourages a sense of closure, a sense that what is found in a text has been finalized, has reached a state of completion. ...By isolating thought in a written

surface, detached from any interlocutor, making utterance in this sense autonomous and indifferent to attack, writing presents utterance and thought as uninvolved with all else, somehow self-contained, complete... The printed text is supposed to represent the words of an author in definitive or "final" form... Once a letterpress forme is closed, locked up, ...the text does not accommodate changes (erasures, insertions)... Print creates a sense of closure not just in literary works but also in analytical philosophical and scientific works... By contrast, the memorable statements of oral cultures and of residually oral manuscripts cultures tended to be of proverbial sort, presenting not 'facts' but rather reflections, often of a gnomic kind, inviting further reflections by the paradoxes they involved." [31]

BOXED CONTENT took the place
of EVANESCENT EVENT

"Writing was an attempt to turn living thoughts dwelling in the human mind into mere objects in the physical world." [32]

Spoken language does not consist of signs, but of events – it takes time. An event cannot be carried around; it simply happens. *"It relies on sound, which is evanescent, having meaning only when it is going out of existence."* [33] *"The concept of 'sign' by contrast, derives*

---

[31] Excerpt from "Orality and Literacy, The technologizing of the world" (Ong, 1988)

[32] Excerpt from Wikipedia's "Orality" entry. (Orality, 2009)

[33] Excerpt from "Writing Electronically : The Effects of Computers on Traditional Writing" by S.P.Ferris (Ferris, 2002)

primarily not from the world of events, but from the world of vision. A sign can be physically carried around, an event cannot." [34]

AUTHORIAL AUTHORITY took the place
of COLLECTIVE CREATION

The printed media has permanence and history while the spoken word is short-lived. Oral societies, having limited capacity to store information, live in the present, adjusting memories that no longer have relevance. Stories that shape people's sense of the world are not frozen in print. They have no authoritative versions, assuming different forms as they are passed through generations, changing with every retelling or re-singing.

[35]

Here are the fifteen...

...oops...

I mean, the TEN commandments

© Orestes Carvalho for the site: Shadows Revolutions

Figure 5: The printed media has permanence and history while the spoken word is short-lived

[34] See (the life and scholarship of Walter J. Ong, SJ, 2008)

[35] Cartoon inspired in a scene of Mel Brooks' "History of the World – Part I" movie. Watch the scene at youtube: http://www.youtube.com/watch?v=4TAtRCJIqnk&feature=related

Goody and Watt reported one classical example: Ndewura Jakpa, the seventeenth century founder of the state of Gonja (north of Ghana), had seven sons. Each one ruled a territorial division within the state. Six decades later two of the divisions disappeared for various reasons. At this point, there were no more references to seven sons. They had been revised to recount that Jakpa had five sons, and that five divisions were created. Since they had no practical, present purpose, the other two sons and divisions had evaporated.[36]

"The very idea of authorship and of the ownership of original work is integrally connected to the establishment of literate culture (which allows you to keep records of original authorship). Copyright is only possible after copywright, you might say." [37] *Who invented the wheel? The fire? The bronze?*

A LONELY READER took the place
                          of A GROUP OF LISTENERS

Written texts work normally or even ideally with an isolated reader while orality is group oriented. Oral cultures form and favor groups. Writing cultures encourage single readers.

---

[36] This example comes from Jack Goody and Ian Watt: "The consequences of literacy" (1968, page 33). It is cited by Ong in his book "Orality and Literacy: The Technologizing of the World" on page 48 (Ong, 1988)

See "General Introduction to the postmodern" (Felluga, 2003)

INDIVIDUAL ABSTRACTION took the place
of PRAGMATIC and EMPATHETIC PARTICIPATION

"Writing presupposes distance in time and space between author and reader." The author creates and packs the knowledge. The reader consumes it, preferably alone, as he or she finds a silent place to read. *"Writing separates us one from another, the knower from the known." "Writing, and especially print, encourages distance, objectivity, and impartiality."* The author has the opportunity to erase, edit and rearrange the words, organizing the flow. With no more limitations of memory, abstract thoughts gain terrain over the immediacy and pragmatism. *"Individualism becomes thinkable, practicable, and encouraged by the solitary experience of either writing or reading the printed page."* [38]

On the other hand, oral societies require a collective experience where the sound of talking surrounds and bonds speaker and listener, where speaker and audience interact to such an extent that all become active participants, listeners and co-creators. *"The spoken word knits people together into community."* [39]

In oral societies people live in close, intimate connection with their environment and each other as they learn trough apprenticeship, observation and practice. They tend not to think in abstract ways about their world and their lives. *"To qualify for storage,*

---

[38] See "How the Secondary Orality of the Electronic Age Can Awaken Us to the Primary Orality of Antiquity," Robert Fowler. (Fowler, 1994)
[39] Ibid.

information must usually concern immediate and practical matters." [40]

"Aleksandr R. Luria, a Soviet psychologist, published a study based on interviews conducted in the nineteen-thirties with illiterate and newly literate peasants in Uzbekistan and Kyrgyzstan. Luria found that illiterates had a 'graphic-functional' way of thinking that seemed to vanish as they were schooled. In naming colors, for example, literate people said 'dark blue' or 'light yellow,' but illiterates used metaphorical names like 'liver,' 'peach,' 'decayed teeth,' and 'cotton in bloom.' Literates saw optical illusions; illiterates sometimes didn't. Experimenters showed peasants drawings of a hammer, a saw, an axe, and a log and then asked them to choose the three items that were similar. Illiterates resisted, saying that all the items were useful. If pressed, they considered throwing out the hammer; the situation of chopping wood seemed more cogent to them than any conceptual category. One peasant, informed that someone had grouped the three tools together, discarding the log, replied, 'Whoever told you that must have been crazy,' and another suggested, 'Probably he's got a lot of firewood." [41]

---

[40] See Wikipedia's "Orality" entry. (Orality, 2009)
[41] See "The Twilight of the Books" by Caleb Crain at The New Yorker, Dec'07 (Crain, 2007)

ANALYTICAL, LINEAR, HIERARCHICAL thought took the place of AGGREGATIVE, REDUNDANT, non-HIERARCHICAL.

In oral language the *"synergy between the body and the construction of oral thought further fuels memory... To solve effectively the problem of retaining and retrieving carefully articulated thought, you have to do your thinking in mnemonic patterns, shaped for ready oral recurrence. Your thoughts must come into being in heavily rhythmic, balanced patterns, in repetitions or antithesis, in alliterations or assonances, in epithetic and other formulary expressions... Serious thought is intertwined with memory systems... Speech that repeat earlier thoughts helps to keep speaker and listener focused on the topic and makes it easier to recall all points later..."* [42]

"With print, words on a page begin to be organized according to a hierarchical logic. Levels of subordination begin to appear, signaled visually by typography. The printed page lends itself to analysis – it can be broken apart into discrete, independent components in a manner that would be impossible and pointless in oral, formulaic, mnemonic speech." [43]

Writing promotes analytical precision and reflective thinking. *"The break from total reliance on oral communication allows people to become more introspective, rational, and individualistic. Abstract thought develops. From the circular world of sound with*

---

[42] See Wikipedia's "Orality" entry. (Orality, 2009)

[43] See "How the Secondary Orality of the Electronic Age Can Awaken Us to the Primary Orality of Antiquity," Robert Fowler. (Fowler, 1994)

its round huts and round villages, people move, over time, toward linear, cause-and-effect thinking, grid-like cities, and a one-thing-at-a-time and one-thing-after-another, and take-time-to-think world that mimics the linear lines of writing and type." [44]

INVESTIGATIVE and CONCILIATORY MINDSET took the place of CONSERVATIVE and
                    AGONISTICALLY TONED MINDSET.

Orality is conservative. *"Storage of information, being primarily dependent on individual or collective recall, must be handled with particular frugality. This creates incentive to avoid exploring new ideas and particularly to avoid the burden of having to store them. It does not prevent oral societies from demonstrating dynamism and change, but there is a premium on ensuring that changes cleave to traditional formulas, and "are presented as fitting the traditions of the ancestors."* [45]

Writing is more rational, less emotional, and more conciliatory. *"Writing disengage humans from direct, interpersonal struggle. Oral literatures from Homer to Beowolf, from Mwindo epic to the Old Testament, are extremely violent by modern standards. They are also punctuated by frequent and intense intellectual combat and tongue-lashings on the one hand, and effusive praise (perhaps reaching its height among African praise singers) on the other."* [46]

---

[44] See the book (page 17) "No Sense of Place - The Impact of Electronic Media on Social Behavior " from Joshua Meyrowitz. (Meyrowitz, 1986)

[45] See Wikipedia's "Orality" entry. (Orality, 2009)

[46] Ibid.

Surf at the Main Sources:

"The life and scholarship of Walter J.Ong" at Saint Louis University site.(http://www.slu.edu/colleges/AS/ENG/ong/influence.html)

"WRITING ELECTRONICALLY: The Effects of Computers on Traditional Writing" by Sharmila Pixy Ferris (http://quod.lib.umich.edu/cgi/t/text/text-idx?c=jep;view=text;rgn=main;idno=3336451.0008.104)

"General Introduction to the Postmodern" by Prof.D.Felluga (http://www.cla.purdue.edu/english/theory/postmodernism/modules/intromainframe.html)

"Orality" at Wikipedia – this one presents a good summary from Walter J. Ong book "Orality and Literacy: The Technologizing of the Word"

"How the Secondary Orality" by R.M.Fowler at (http://homepages.bw.edu/~rfowler/pubs/secondoral/index.html) – this is a MUST READ; specially the chapter "From Orality to Literacy to Hypertext: Back to the Future?" It has a very clever and foresighted analysis, which address the current chapter discussions as well as the next chapter: "Back to the Village"

"Changing Media, Changing Us" page – which inspired the title of this chapter – within Cybermedia site by Mindy McAdams (http://mindymcadams.com/cybermedia/meyrowitz.html) (McAdams, 1999)

THREE

Back to the Village

In this chapter we connect the changes fostered by the print medium – stated in the chapter two – to the changes happening at the beginning of this twenty-first century driven by the digital medium. Once we escape the short-term myopia of our literate paradigms we begin to identify the underlying factors leading to the current changes.

> **Suddenly we see ourselves back to the old village. But it is an old village on steroids, where our memory and our reach have been multiplied manifold. The post-literate society is becoming a "hyper-oral" society.**

A medium affects the society in which it plays a role not only by the content delivered over the medium, but by the characteristics of the medium itself.

From Wikipedia's entry about Marshall McLuhan's phrase:
"The medium is the message"

And as the prevalent medium in our society change, so changes our society.

Marshal McLuhan pointed out how the dominant medium traits rather than its content have the power to shape people's way of thinking and behavior. *"The medium is the message,"* he said. And he foresaw the changes triggered by the new electronic mediums when he coined the term

"Global Village" in his 1962s book "The Gutenberg Galaxy." (See box about it below)

> ### The Gutenberg Galaxy
>
> The Gutenberg Galaxy: The Making of Typographic Man is a book by Marshall McLuhan, in which he analyzes the effects of mass media, especially the printing press, on European culture and human consciousness. It popularized the term global village, which refers to the idea that mass communication allows a village-like mindset to apply to the entire world; and Gutenberg Galaxy, which we may regard today to refer to the accumulated body of recorded works of human art and knowledge, especially books.
>
> McLuhan studies the emergence of what he calls Gutenberg Man, the subject produced by the change of consciousness wrought by the advent of the printed book. Apropos of his axiom, "The medium is the message," McLuhan argues that technologies are not simply inventions which people employ but are the means by which people are re-invented. The invention of movable type was the decisive moment in the change from a culture in which all the senses partook of a common interplay to a tyranny of the visual. He also argued that the development of the printing press led to the creation of nationalism, dualism, domination of rationalism, automatisation of scientific research, uniformation and standardisation of culture and alienation of individuals.
>
> See "The Gutenberg Galaxy" article at Wikipedia

For many centuries paper was the dominant medium shaping the literate societies way of thinking, social organization and behavior. Then came the radio waves carrying the sounds, and the TV waves broadcasting movies and programs. McLuhan talked about the changes such new mediums were nurturing in our civilization.

Walter J. Ong, a McLuhan disciple, noted that after moving from oral societies to literate societies we were now moving to post-literate societies getting into what he called a secondary orality which *"is founded on – though it departs from – the individualized introversion of the age of writing and print and rationalism which intervened between it and primary orality which remains as part of us."* [47]

> **People are looking to their peers - instead of looking for authorities - and decisions and solutions are surfacing from the bottom.**

But McLuhan's Global Village basic idea – heavily based upon mass communication media – and Ong's secondary orality – also fed by the new mediums: TV and radio – are still locked into literate paradigms. Both are still dependent on the rationalism and analytical discourse that comes from print. They are still locked into the sense of closure, the authorial authority of mass communication. They still rest on the organizations and habits of writing, because those electronic mediums are still into Gutenberg's mass production one-to-many model. Even though these new twenty-first century mediums were adding elements of orality to the "written word world" they weren't yet much close to the old village orality, to the many-to-many conversation mode, where the thoughts and the truth were built collectively. They were still locked into one-owns-the-truth, no-changes-anymore because we are ready-to-produce-and-distribute-to-the-masses mode.

---

[47] See "Rhetoric, Romance, and Technology" by W.J.Ong, page 285 (Ong, Rhetoric, Romance, and Technology, 1971)

Nevertheless McLuhan and Ong provided the foundation that helps us understand the impact of digital technology. They saw the implications of new electronic mediums and how they were pushing us back in a secondary orality. They also saw the birth of the digital medium but unfortunately they didn't live enough to see its consequences in full bloom, which we start to see now, after the fog of the Internet bubble burst dissipated.

Take the authorial authority. This is a requirement in the literate society. You can't print – or broadcast – everyone's ideas. You need to select one idea – at least for that printing batch – and this one will dominate the truth until it can be refuted in a future article or book. You also need to close it. You can't keep changing it as you learn more about it. Once you print it; it is done.

But with the digital medium you "literally" can listen to everyone's idea and you can keep building on it. There is no need to close it anymore.

As we think about this, we start to see the strong limitations books have. We start to see some reason behind that Duke student's statement: *"We don't read whole books anymore."*[48] Books can be very interesting, but they also can be boringly linear, authoritative and slow, even more for digital natives raised in the increasing rate of increasing speed, multilayered, multiple lines of action, world of the videogames. *"These aspects are all foreign to the one-thing-at-a-time, one-thing-after-another, and take-time-to-think world of reading."*[49]

---

[48] See Preface – "Writing a Book about the End of Books"
[49] See page 326 of Joshua Meyrowitz book "No Sense of Place - The Impact of Electronic Media on Social Behavior " (Meyrowitz, 1986)

As stated in the chapter two: books are somewhat out of synch with thought. They are slow. They have limited scope – they can reach just one person at a time. Books also put people apart as they presuppose distance in time and space between author and reader. Books disengage humans from direct, interpersonal discussion. It is a solitary task. A text can't debate with someone.

But digital technology and the Internet are overcoming such limitations, putting the best of oral and literate worlds together. In this new era we can have the long-standing memory and the reach from the literate world coupled with the engagement and debates from the oral world. We can have a lot more than a book can deliver.

Therefore it is reasonable to think that the author role and the traditional book will change. Maybe the question is not IF the books – as we know them – will be gone one day, but how long will it take. Fifty years? Or less? [50]

What about linearity and hierarchies?

Writing and reading require them. Literate society lives in a model of one-to-many – of authorial authority, editorial filtering.

However the hypertext is anything but linear and the control is on consumer's hands. We build our experience and we build our perspective on the truth or on what we read, see, and listen, the way we want, when we surf through the Internet. The Internet throws us back into a

---

[50] Take a look at these two interesting articles addressing this subject: "The Twilight of the Book" by Caleb Crain, The New Yorker, Dec '07 and "Out of Print: The death and life of American newspaper" by Eric Alterman, The New Yorker, Mar '08 (Alterman, 2008)

many-to-many conversation model, as in the old village, where the dialogue is always open and more people can participate.

We then ask: how will this affect social organization and hierarchies? Will we still need in the future – long term or not – representatives in the congress to make decisions in our name?

Perhaps not far in the future the entire population will be able to make the decisions by themselves (many-to-many style) or through some mechanism where people can have more participation on the issues that matter most to them – like a wiki (see appendix to this chapter about Wikis). This is somehow already happening in the Internet (we will talk more about that in the epilogue) where people are already looking to their peers – instead of looking for authorities – and decisions and solutions are surfacing from the bottom.

What about private organizations? How much of the middle manager functions are related to filtering information and making it more manageable in the old one-to-many style? The borders between corporations and free market are about to be radically redefined.

· · ·

"History doesn't repeat itself but it often rhymes."[51]

---

[51] Mark Twain

Authorial-authority, linearity, hierarchies... We can see the bubbles forming inside the pot. From our blind spot inside the rapidly heating water we start to see some rhymes. (Do you remember the boiling pot in chapter one – Unnoticed Revolutions?)

When we learn about the influence that the dominant medium can exert over different societies, when we look farther back in time, to the oral societies in the old villages, we have an enlightening experience. We start to recognize the tune that is playing at the beginning of this twenty-first century. We see rhymes of deeper changes than the changes that a simple technology life cycle, or a clash of generations would bring. We see rhymes of changes that can affect profoundly our civilization – the way we think and the way we organize ourselves. We see ourselves back to the old village. But now, it is an old village on steroids, where our memory and our reach have been multiplied manifold.

As in the old village we don't need any longer to close the thought and get "ready-to-publish." We don't need also the authorial authority backed by its pretense of truth. We can maintain online discussions with millions and we can collaboratively build robust ever-evolving ideas.

As in the old village we don't need any more an editorial filter deciding for us what is worth reading, watching or hearing. We can decide by ourselves – or at least we can have a filter tailored specifically for us not for the masses.

As in the old village we can know the people's reputations – but now of millions – as if we have been gossiping about them for years.

The old author-thought, one-way, one-to-many hierarchical mass communication flow is giving way to a new collaborative-thought, multiple-ways, many-to-many networked flow. **The post-literate society is becoming a "hyper-oral society."**

. . .

Changing Again

From reading manuscripts out loud to the introspective experience of printed books. Now this experience is changing again as the digital medium takes over.

"Ask people who learned to read before the Internet what they liked about the experience, and they'll talk to you about taking books to the beach or up in trees to read, reading late at night by flashlight under the bedcovers, loving the smell of paper and glue, delighting to hold in their hands a new book for its freshness or a used book for its mystery, and paying unusually close attention to the dried flowers or love notes or news clippings they used for bookmarks. Those pleasures are lost to readers of this page. In return, you get the choice to follow or ignore hyperlinks, surprising images in vibrant color, and (if I were more a resource intensive web writer) music and full-motion video..."

from <u>Manuscript to Print</u> at Goucher College site. (Sanders)

"We shape our tools then our tools shape us." [52]

---

[52] Marshal McLuhan

BACK TO THE VILLAGE

Oral Societies	Literate Societies	Hyper-oral Societies	
Ever changing thought	vs. Feeling of Closure	vs. Back to Conversation	Blogs, forums, wikis and fluid flow of information through links and hypertext.
Evanescent Event	vs. Boxed Content	vs. Ever changing experience	Content gives way to services, debates, dynamic real time mash ups.
Collective Creation	vs. Authorial authority	vs. Collective Creation	Open source, wikis, mash ups, collaboration, create on the go depending on each participant action
Group of Listener	vs. Lonely Reader	vs. Online Communities	Forums, chat rooms, IM, Twitter, Social Networks
Pragmatic, Empathetic Participation	vs. Individual Abstraction	vs. Communal Participation	New civic sphere where people build ad-hoc communities. Pragmatic. Bottom up surveillance.
Aggregative, Redundant, non-hierarchical thought	vs. Analytical, Linear and Hierarchical thought	vs. Aggregative, Parallel, Networked thought	Mash ups, Hyperlink jumps, collaborative creations, collective interpretations.
Conservative and Agonistically toned	vs. Investigative and Conciliatory	vs. Engagement	Back to personal debates and struggles, but without memory limitations

Table 2: Back to the Village - From Oral to Literate to Hyper-oral

Wikis

Participative bottom-up creation vs. top-down authoritative design

Wikis are a good example of the power of the "Back to the Village" rhyme. Freed from literate paradigms such as authorial authority, feeling of closure, privacy and hierarchies, wikis are a remarkable expression of the hyper-oral society. In this appendix we use wikis example to discuss, under the light of "back to the village" metaphor, some key concerns of this new digital era. What was the role of reputation at the old villages? Were they egalitarian? Isn't privacy a concept of literate-mass-media era? Does innovation come more often from individual abstraction or from participative debates?

A Wiki is a database composed by web pages that allows the visitors to easily add, remove and edit its pages. Although a wiki goes beyond "allowing" visitors to change their pages. It "requests" visitors to do changes because the whole database is built based on visitors input.

This is a radical departure from traditional assemblage of knowledge, which is more related to a top-down design while wikis are closer to a bottom-up Darwinian approach.

The simplicity and openness of the wikis cause many people to reject the idea. They assume the wiki will eventually become garbage if anyone can edit it without restrictions:

- *What if the person doing the typing has no idea what he or she is talking about?*

- *What if the person is a vandal and inserts profanity?*

- *What if the person is a vandal and either completely erases the page or corrupts it?*

While it does happen, that kind of thing is relatively rare. The key component that makes a wiki work is its community. Using a variety of tools the community sees to it that vandals, dummies and spammers do not corrupt the encyclopedia.[53]

Wikis work because changes to the wiki pages go through a natural selection process:

- Changes that add up to the community knowledge base (people agree) remains as part of the wiki.

- Changes that go against the community knowledge are naturally eliminated. The community corrects it.

- Previous versions of the page are kept in the database with the name or IP address of the person who accomplished the change.

There are a few mechanisms that can accelerate such selection process. A key one is that people who contributed to build a page can be automatically notified when that page changes, so they can evaluate whether they agree or not with the change. This way people discuss and improve the piece of the knowledge-base they care most about, what leads to higher involvement and higher quality.

---

[53] See "How Wikis Work" by Marshal Brain (Brain)

Wikis are spreading throughout the web, including corporate intranets.[54] Not all have the same mechanisms, rules and the same openness. But the principle is the same: bottom-up participative assemblage of knowledge.

The results can be surprisingly good for the skeptics. To put the process to test the journal Nature did a study comparing the accuracy of a sample of articles from Encyclopedia Britannica and Wikipedia (probably the most known wiki).

Nature's experts found 123 errors in the former and 162 in the latter – one astonishing result for the totally open Wikipedia which has been built by hundreds of thousands of contributors and already has 12 times more articles than the entire printed version of Britannica.[55]

Nevertheless, despite the surprising result – which Britannica dispute [56] – Wikipedia has some serious flaws.

One of its main issues is that it tries to be egalitarian. This means a teenager with little knowledge about a specific subject but with enough passion and available time can overturn the contributions of a scholar who has dedicated his life to that same specific subject. It happens often. The researcher finds an error in an article related to a topic within his or her area of expertise. The researcher decides to contribute and spend some good amount of time rewriting the article just to find out later, someone has changed the article back to its original version. The researcher corrects it again just to see it getting back, one

---

[54] See "No Rest for the Wiki" by R.King,, Business Week (King, 2007)
[55] See "The Wiki Principle," (Economist, The wiki principle, 2006d)
[56] Britannica's refuted Nature's article through an online letter: http://corporate.britannica.com/britannica_nature_response.pdf and Nature's responded back saying they won't retract the article: http://www.nature.com/press_releases/Britannica_response.pdf

more time, to its original flawed version. The researcher gives up and leaves. The teenager stays, victoriously guarding his or her shallow and misinformed point of view. Such mechanism ends up filtering out reputable contributors from the whole community, overrating passionate teenagers that have plenty of free time.[57] Ironically, because it is trying to be egalitarian, Wikipedia incurs the risk of become a community of equals dominated by teenagers and therefore having a knowledge base that reflects the knowledge of such community.

This kind of issue has been moving the general perception of Wikipedia (and other wikis) from an outstanding success to a total flop. [58]

As in all new concepts, the initial phase of inflated expectations is followed by disillusionment until the technology stabilizes and people realize the actual value of the idea.   [59]

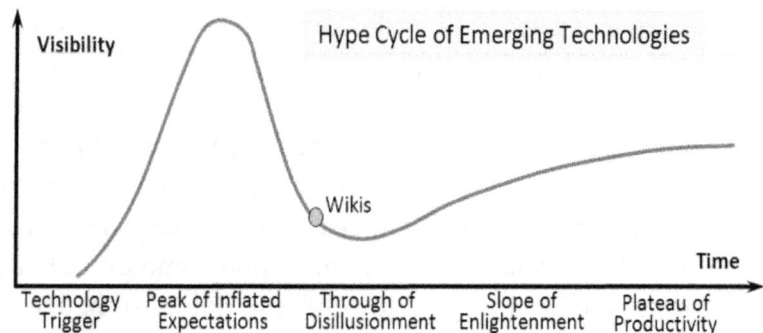

Figure 6: Emerging technologies cycle – Wikis (Majchrzak, 2007)

[57] See "Why Wikipedia Can't Work" by Charles Cazabon. (Cazabon)
[58] See "Do problems with Wikipedia presage social networking's end?" by Paul Murphy (Murphy, 2008) See also "Sand Castles of Knowledge" by Kyle Gann, May'07.
[59] Chart based on "The Promise of Passion of Collective Wisdom through Wikis" by Ann Majchrzak, InThink Network, 2007 (Majchrzak, 2007)

Wikipedia flaws have been used as an example of the limitations of peer production, the limitation of the crowd's wisdom and the need of hierarchies, authorial authorities and editorial filters. Nicholas Carr writes in his article "The Ignorance of the Crowds:"[60]

> But if peer production is a good way to mine the raw material for innovation, it doesn't seem well suited to shaping that material into a final product. That's a task that is still best done in the closed quarters of a cathedral [hierarchy], where a relatively small and formally organized group of talented professionals can collaborate closely in perfecting the fit and finish of a product. Involving a crowd in this work won't speed it up; it will just bring delays and confusion.

Carr's criticism reflects the old tension between free markets and hierarchies where coordination costs determine what stays within closed quarters and what goes to the market defining the borders of one company. But he underestimates the role of the crowd and overstates the prescience of the talent.

Consider the whole Internet, for example. Who or which company or which organized group of professionals created it? Did it come from an intelligent design or it is more a result of a bottom-up Darwinian creation?

The lonely genius is a myth, wrote James Burke.[61] *"In the history of scientific and technological endeavor, there are few if any cases in which the end was exactly what was*

---

[60] See "The Ignorance of the Crowd" by Nicholas Carr, Summer'07 (Carr, 2007)
[61] See "Inventors & Inventions" by J.Burke, Dec'00 at Time site. (Burke, 2000)

intended at the beginning." Throughout history, scientific discoveries and innovations came as a consequence of an interconnected web of knowledge, people and events transcending any closed quarter. [62]

But no matter Wikipedia's flaws, no matter the concerns related to the limitations of peer production, wikis and collaborative technologies are moving to the mainstream. Executives in many companies are already considering the next step in the trend towards more open innovation. [63]

Still, probably the main issue with Wikipedia and also with the critics against Wikipedia is that both are somehow stuck in the old literate-mass-media paradigm. They still think in terms of content. They still think in terms of packing information, making it a final product, closing the package and distributing it to the masses. This is what encyclopedias do. Shadows in a box. A monolithic inert authoritative monologue placed inside a box and distributed to the masses. It could be argued that Wikipedia is about participation. That's right, but when it tries to build an encyclopedia by the masses to the masses, it risks end up building a huge mass monologue.

"The old media model was: there is one source of truth. The new media model is: there are multiple sources of truth, and we will sort it out." [64]

---

[62] See more about this discussion on open-collaborative vs. "closed quarters" innovation in chapter seven.

[63] See "The next step in open innovation" by J.Bughin, M.Chui and B.Johnson, at The McKinsey Quaterly, Jun 2008. (Bughin, Chui, & Johnson, 2008)

[64] Joe Kraus, the founder of JotSpot quoted at "Among the Audience" at The Economiste, Apr'06 (Among the audience, 2006)

The new village is no longer about monologues. It is about conversations. Instead of from-me-to-you, it is from-us-to-us, building it together. It is not about consensus, but about debate. It is about understanding the different points of view of every thinker as well as the thinker reputation.

And villages are not egalitarian. Egalitarian societies only exist in the primitive form of the hunter-gatherers' bands or in the mind of an intelligent designer. The wisdom of the crowd taught us that people are different from each other and therefore they should be treated differently.

> " Lack of privacy is not a bug, but a feature of the network.

So, in a conversation, not only what is being said matters, but also the reputation of the one who is saying it. And the whole exchange will affect not only the overall knowledge about the discussion's subject but it will also affect the reputation of the participants. They are all interconnected and cannot be put apart. One of the main reasons people participate is to build their reputations. People's reputations in turn are a key element when we weigh up their contributions.

Reputation was extremely important in the old villages. It determined the person's ability to buy or to sell and to reap the benefits of trust and reciprocal respect.

Anonymity is a modern print-mass-culture innovation that is being reverted now as we leave behind us the first wild years of total anonymity – playing with identities – in the Internet. Clive Thompson wrote about this change:[65]

---

[65] See "Brave New World of Digital Intimacy" by Clive Thompson at The New York Times, Sep'08. (Thompson, 2008)

"It's just like living in a village, where it's actually hard to lie because everybody knows the truth already," Tufekci said. [Zeynep Tufeckci is a sociologist at the University of Maryland]   "The current generation is never unconnected. They're never losing touch with their friends. So we're going back to a more normal place, historically. If you look at human history, the idea that you would drift through life, going from new relation to new relation, that's very new. It's just the 20th century."

Psychologists and sociologists spent years wondering how humanity would adjust to the anonymity of life in the city, the wrenching upheavals of mobile immigrant labor — a world of lonely people ripped from their social ties. We now have precisely the opposite problem. Indeed, our modern awareness tools reverse the original conceit of the Internet. When cyberspace came along in the early '90s, it was celebrated as a place where you could reinvent your identity — become someone new.

"If anything, it's identity-constraining now," Tufekci told me... "You know that old cartoon? 'On the Internet, nobody knows you're a dog'? On the Internet today, everybody knows you're a dog! If you don't want people to know you're a dog, you'd better stay away from a keyboard."

See "Brave New World of Digital Intimacy"
(Thompson, 2008).

"Privacy is not an Option," Aaron Schmidt wrote in his blog: [66]

> When talking about social software, especially MySpace and Facebook, I get asked about privacy a lot. It often goes like this: "What are these people doing sharing this information about themselves!? Anyone can look at it! Oh.My.God!" And I often feel like saying, "Duh, that's the point." This is not a bug on the web, it is a feature. They also know that to a certain extent, fully participating in the 21st century means forgetting about privacy.

It will still take some time until we get rid of our old paradigms. We are just learning how to build the new villages. We are just learning how to participate and how to manage our online reputation.

No matter what, Wikipedia initiative exemplifies the huge power to be harnessed from the crowd. It garnered a few million voluntary editors[67] and it has been growing at a vertiginous pace. *"In the month of July 2006, Wikipedia grew by over thirty million words. At a rate of six hundred words a minute, twenty four hours a day, a person could read nearly twenty seven million words in a month. In other words, a sleepless fast reader could never catch up with Wikipedia's new content."*[68]

---

[66] See "Privacy is not an Option" at Aaron Schmidt blog(Schmidt, 2007)
[67] See "Who Writes Wikipedia?" by Aaron Swartz, (Swartz, 2006)
[68] See Wikipedia at Wikipedia

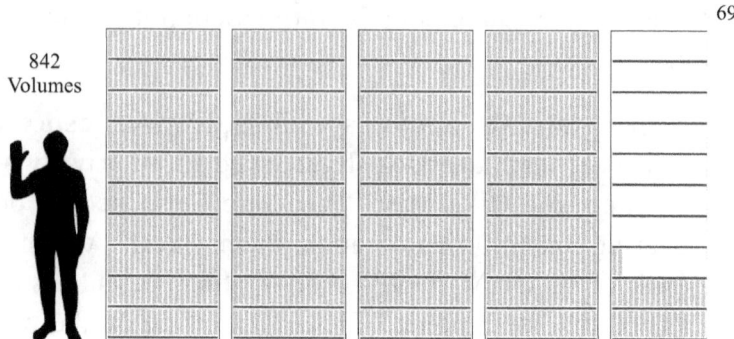

Figure 7: Wikipedia size if printed in books

In July 2007 Wikipedia accounted for a *"a staggering one out of every 200 page views on the entire Internet."* [70]

Wikis will get better when they find the right equation to balance the contributions of the community members with those members reputation. Rather than hierarchical structures and editorial filters we will probably find out what matter most is who the wiki attracts to its community and what is the level of engagement of its members. Because a wiki is nothing more than an expression of its community; an expression of the village.

"This is the ultimate effect of the new awareness: It brings back the dynamics of small-town life, where everybody knows your business." [71]

---

[69] See Wikipedia entry at Wikipedia
[70] See "All the News That's Fit to Print Out" by Jonathan Dee, New York Times Jul'07 (Dee, 2007)
[71] See "Brave New World of Digital Intimacy" (Thompson, 2008)

FOUR

The Print Mold and the Mass Media Era

This chapter shows how the changes driven by the dominance of the print medium are intertwined with the dominance of the mass production and the mold concept: one design, one mold and countless replications. These concepts have driven an outstanding increase in productivity and wealth. The mass production idea has put an army of fantastic machines working for us. General people got access to books and information we never had before. Our knowledge got broader but also more uniform as it was shaped by the same mold. The mold with its economies of scale and each medium technology erected business empires and kept them in silos protected from competition. But now the digital medium is breaking down these silos.

Progress has made our life more complex. Trains, airplanes, computers, many and many bills, TV, newspapers, traffic and tight schedules make us wish sometimes we could have a simpler life.

However, progress also made our life much easier than it used to be at Early Middle Ages.

The manor, a large estate that included the manor house, pastures, fields, and a village, became the economic unit of the early Middle Ages...

...Because no central authority or organized trade existed, each manor tried to be self-sufficient, or able to produce everything it needed. Most manors produced their own food, clothing, and leather goods. Only a few items – such as iron, salt, tar, or wine – were purchased.

... A typical manor village, usually on a stream that furnished waterpower for its mill, had houses clustered together for safety, a short distance away from the manor house or castle. The land of the manor extended out from the village and included vegetable plots, cultivated fields, pastures, and forests...

Long hours spent doing backbreaking work in the fields made daily life on a manor very hard.

The laborers' meager diet consisted mainly of coarse black bread, cabbage and a few other vegetables, cheese, and eggs... People rarely ate meat because they needed animals to help them work the fields and because they were not allowed to hunt on the lord's land...

The life of ordinary people was brief and narrow in medieval times. Because of disease, starvation, and constant warfare, the average life expectancy was about 30 years. Since people in their forties were regarded as very old, medieval society was a much younger society than ours. Ordinary people rarely escaped the village. They usually died where they had been born.

See "World History, People and Nations, Ancient World,"
(Holt, 2000)

The Birth of Mass Production

The Gutenberg bible was one of the first mass manufactured products in this world. The paper was the first mass medium. The model – one to many instead of one to one – was much more productive. It opened the frontiers for other mass productions that came – clothes, automobiles, electronics. Somehow, all evolved into the same standardized, productivity centric model: one design – mass production – mass communication – mass distribution.

Mass production dramatically reduced the costs of a book – and all other Industrial age products – making them affordable and accessible to most of the population.

Basically the model works this way: instead of spending your time scribing the books one by one; you first spend a good amount of your time, or money, building equipment that will automate the process. Once you have the equipment, you can produce hundreds of identical books for a fraction of the time and cost you faced before. Now you need to sell as many copies as possible in order to recover the investment – time and money – you did building the equipment. If you sell just a few books, you've lost your time and money building the equipment. If you sell a large number, you get rich, and you can build even better equipment that works faster and better, making you even richer.

In order to sell such large number, you need as many people as possible aware of the product you have; you need mass advertising. You also need to be able to deliver to all those people, even beyond your village. You need mass distribution. The same logic applies to your mass advertising and mass distribution. If you go tell people one by one about the book you are selling, it will take you a long time to reach enough people. Better if you can put a message in a newspaper.

You will not be able to deliver many books if you walk to your buyers delivering your books one by one. You do better investing on a distribution system – buying trucks, hiring drivers – or having another company doing it for you.

This has been the model that put incredible machines working for us and raised the standard of living at a level that old villages' people would never be able to imagine.

Mass Media Zenith

> "People had never known so much, and their knowledge had never been so homogeneous, because it was made prisoner of the same mold.

A few centuries after the printing press, Thomas Edison invented how to record sounds in a vinyl disc and soon a whole industry of huge companies was also built around that. Following this path, a whole "Media Sector" was formed, composed of large industries, each around a different medium – books, newspaper, magazines, photographic paper, radio waves, TV air waves, cables, film movies, vinyl discs, etc., – each following approximately the same model:

1st-Capture thoughts, sounds or images, put them inside a medium and make them a product;

2nd-Mass produce this product;

3rd-Create mass awareness of it;

4th-Mass distribute it;

5th-Sell devices to play it. From simple reading glasses to expensive home theaters;

6th-Pocket tons of money and re-feed the model.

This has been a win-win model. It worked great for general people who got access to information and entertainment that they wouldn't be able to get other ways. It worked great for the companies. The better the companies did on satisfying the general public, the more money they made and larger they got.

And they became stronger and stronger dominating the means of production and the means of distribution. Newspapers for example dominated the whole "printed news" cycle, from creation (through their teams of reporters) to aggregation of news (through their editors) to production (in their printing presses) to door-to-door distribution. For a good amount of years, their content couldn't be found anywhere else than in their printed piece of paper.

The 500-year-old model reached its zenith probably at the second half of the twentieth century when most adult Americans were simultaneously turning on their television sets to watch "I Love Lucy." [72]

At that point general people had never known so much, and their knowledge had never been so homogeneous, because it was made prisoner of the same mold. People were following, like cattle, the editors' choices and the authors' pretense truths.

---

[72] See "Among the Audience", (Among the audience, 2006). See also "The Rise and Fall of the Hit" by Chris Anderson, at Wired Magazine, Jul'06. (Anderson, 2006)

Silo walls – the medium and the economics of scale

Back to that book manufacturing: as you make more money, you buy better equipment, you sell even more books, you spend more in advertising, you improve your distribution, you hire people and your company gets huge.

As your company gets bigger, it gets harder and harder for anyone else to set up another company to compete against you. They would need to take a big risk on building or buying all the machines you already have, building a distribution system as efficient as yours, and setting up all the workflows you've already put in place along the years to deal with your huge volumes.

Your big company owns the means of production and the means of distribution, and nobody knows better than you how to print thoughts in a book or how to put music in a vinyl disc or how to put a TV show on airwaves, and how to sell them to the masses. Your economies of scale, the knowledge and investment you have accumulated on dealing with your medium – paper, vinyl or airwaves – act like silo walls protecting your fort from an alien assault.

The Fall of Mass Media

Up to end of the twentieth century, different media industries – books, newspaper, radio, TV, etc., – grew protected in their silos, having each medium and their economies of scale acting as walls shielding their vertical models – some, like the newspapers, more vertical than others.

But then, a very disruptive technology – a new medium – cracked those silos.

Before digital technology, texts were supposed to be on paper, music on vinyl, movies projected on the big screen coming from a film stock, or projected on a TV screen coming through the airwaves. But now you can have all of them in the same one digital medium.

Before digital technology and before its offspring – the Internet – you had no other option than attach your creation (thoughts, stories, music, text, etc.) to a physical medium before having them distributed to your buyers and consumers. The control was in the hands of the big media companies who had the equipment, the knowledge and the distribution system.

> The content has decoupled from the medium.

But now the content has decoupled from the medium and you can easily throw those creations into the Internet having instant access to millions of potential buyers.

Suddenly we realized that all those products – books, music discs, DVDs, videotapes – which attach information or a mental creation to a medium, are not so physical as our paradigms led us to believe. They are more like shadows-in-the-box.

As a consequence, because the digital technology is releasing the shadows from physical containers, the old mass production model is becoming obsolete. Most of the media industries, which have been dealing with packaging, selling and distributing those shadows are being deeply affected.

The old medium barrier has gone down. With digital medium and widespread Internet, the economics of scale do not apply anymore to the production and the distribution of what media industry usually call content. Media companies are losing control of production and distribution within their medium silos. Ordinary people, as well as companies from other industries, are now able to compete against big media companies, producing and distributing their thoughts, stories, music, still images and videos.

The new digital medium is driving new ways of thinking, behaviors and social structures. Without the need to lock content within a box, the mass-production-distribution, hierarchical, linear, author-created, one-to-many model is giving way to a non-linear, non-hierarchical, group-created, many-to-many, mesh-model that better reflects people real-life social interactions.

And the shadows are escaping from the boxes. The content is giving way to the event, leading to ever changing live experiences or services. Media products are becoming things of the past giving way to media services.

FIVE

Landgrab Fight in the Old Media's Land

In this chapter we see some examples on how the digital medium is bringing down former powerful companies, changing the nature of competition and reshaping the business landscape. We discuss how the old literate-mass-culture paradigm kept most companies blind to the deepness of the current changes.

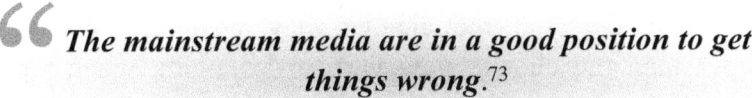 *The mainstream media are in a good position to get things wrong.*[73]

"No question the most insidious virus in our midst is the illegal downloading of music on the Net," said the president and CEO of Recording Academy at the Grammy Awards in 2002. *"This illegal file-sharing and ripping of music files is pervasive, out of control and oh so criminal,"* he added.[74]

At that time – 2002 – the music industry understood something very significant was happening in their industry. They didn't take long to act. They went to court against Napster – a music-sharing site created by Shawn Fanning a

---

[73] David Weinberger "blogger, author and fellow at Harvard University's Berkman Centre" quoted at "Among the Audience" (Among the audience, 2006)

[74] See the **speech of Michael Greene** President and CEO of the Recording Academy during the Grammy Awards Feb. 27, 2002 (Greene, 2002)

19-year-old college dropout – and had it closed. Next step, they put a great amount of energy suing individuals who were engaging in online music file swapping.

The recording industry was right in two points: First, what was happening was very important to their industry; Second, downloading files without buying them was not right, it was illegal.

So they reacted, mostly through legal proceedings trying to make sure people could understand the control should be in their hands not in the hands of general people, artists and consumers.

Nevertheless, they missed the most important point. They couldn't understand the change they were facing "was deeper than the change they had to deal with, when tape recording technology arrived. They couldn't understand that the time of heavy-hand control was over and that their silo walls were collapsing.

> **They couldn't understand that the time of heavy-hand control was over and that their silo walls were collapsing.**

However, somebody else, from a totally different industry, understood it. And at the same moment that the recording industry was focusing their energy on scaring people about sharing music files in the Internet, Apple was launching their iPods and their new music services through iTunes.

"Consumers don't want to be treated like criminals and artists don't want their valuable work stolen," said Apple Chief Executive Officer, Steve Jobs.[75]

---

[75] See "Apple Launches the iTunes Music Store," at Apple Press Releases Library. (Apple, 2003)

He understood the silo was broken. He knew the medium and distribution barriers were down so he could get his company in. He understood music wasn't a physical packaged good, as we tended to believe for so many years; music was an experience. He understood consumers wanted to control, not to be controlled. As a result, in a very short time he not just put his company at the leading edge of what became the new music industry, but his company also became the number one music retailer in US – getting Wal Mart territory off-guard as well.

Top 10 US music retailers: January 2008
Percent

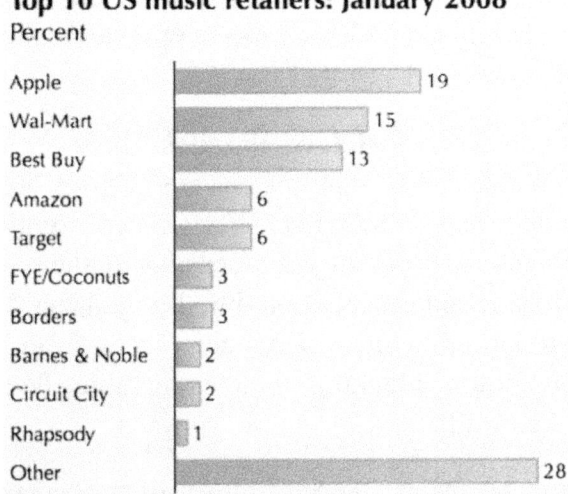

Figure 8: Apple passes Wal-mart, now #1 music retailer in US (Bangeman, 2008)

A few years have passed since Napster was closed. Most media companies had time to learn and be better prepared to outsiders' inroad. But maybe not many companies are prepared yet. Locked to old paradigms and legacy issues, having big streams of their revenue still coming from old business models, it seems some media industry executives couldn't understand yet their piece of responsibility on their industry debacles. In a 2007 speech, NBC Universal CEO Jeff Zucker blamed Apple for destroying the music business and for threatening to do the same in the video industry.[76]

Once again someone in the media industry was looking through the window trying to find out someone to blame, when he would do better looking at the mirror or at his company's consumers, trying to understand the changes triggered by the new digital medium in their consumers behavior and way of thinking.

Apple didn't change the music business alone. The music landscape was already changing, when Apple was smart enough to appreciate it and surf that wave.

The digital media has knocked down the silos. However not all companies realized yet that they were thrown in a landgrab fight in a no man's land. They keep fighting within their old industry paradigms, focusing in their old silo and in their same old competition, blindly ignoring that in this new battleground, the real danger comes from an unexpected competitor attacking their vulnerable flanks through the broken walls.

The next paragraphs bring some examples of movements that are already affecting the old industries landscape.

Cable companies made a powerful raid within the old kingdom of telephone companies. They grabbed some significant land through their triple play offering (TV, Internet and telephone conversations through VoIP – voice delivered over the Internet). By August 2007, Comcast (a

---

[76] See "Apple has destroyed the music business" by David Schatsky, Oct'07.

US cable TV company) was already among the top ten US phone companies: *"With its 2.4 million VoIP lines, Comcast is now in the top 10 of U.S. phone companies by number of lines, and may soon be in the top 5."* [77] By March 2009, Comcast became the third largest residential phone provider in US.[78]

Telecom operators in turn got into TV broadcasting territory deploying a fiber infrastructure that delivers high speed broadband and TV channels. *"Both AT&T and Verizon, which together serve about three-quarters of [US] switched access lines, have begun offering their own video services."*[79]

Wireless carriers are losing their grip on the mobile services industry. Their silo is getting crowded not only by upstarts – like Google[80] and Apple[81] – coming from unrelated industries but also by their traditional partners. For example the mobile device maker Nokia is bypassing the carriers partnering with Skype to provide VoIP. Nokia is also providing many other services like music, mobile games, photos and video sharing.[82]

The same former-computer-company – Apple – that stormed the music industry, also attacked the mobile-device-maker land. In little more than a year after the

---

[77] See "Comcast Overtakes Vonage," Aug'07 at Telecompetitor site. (Telecompetitor, 2007)

[78] See "Comcast is now the 3rd largest U.S. phone company," Mar'09 at Gigaom web site. (GigaOM, 2009)

[79] See "Cable vs. Telco: The Battle Heats up" by Richard Siderman, Oct'07 at Business Week site (Siderman, 2007)

[80] Take a look at Google-Phone site: http://www.google-phone.com/

[81] Apple Iphone site: http://www.apple.com/iphone/

[82] See "Bypassing Carriers for Mobile Content," Apr'08 and "VoIP Goes Mobile," Aug'08 by Olga Kharif at businessweek.com.

iPhone launch Apple was already the third largest mobile phone maker in the world, just behind Nokia and Samsung.[83] And having the iPhone as a Trojan horse Apple inserted itself also in the mobile-service-provider land. Meanwhile it opened another front in the video-entertainment-distribution land renting movies through iTunes and making computer videos accessible at TV screens through Apple TV.

Microsoft also got beyond its original software space getting into game devices, mobile devices and services.

Amazon got into a mobile network operation (carriers kingdom) to deliver content to be read in its "Kindle" electronic device (electronic manufacturers' kingdom).

In this new world there are no more exclusive turfs. The land is up for grabs. The companies that understood the changes, brought by the digital media, are reviewing their purpose and scope. They are adjusting as fast as they can. But it is not easy to turn a big ship, especially when a company has a big amount of its profit streams coming out of the old model.

Motorola has one slide from an investor meeting presentation that represents how this landgrab fight is affecting their industries:[84]

---

[83] See "Earnings Call: Jobs Says iPhone Revs Total $4.6B, Making Apple the Third-Largest Handset Maker" by Tricia Duryee, at paidcontent.org, Oct'21 (Duryee, 2008)

[84] See Motorola's "2007 Financial Analyst Meeting Presentation" at Motorola's website. (Moloney, 2007)

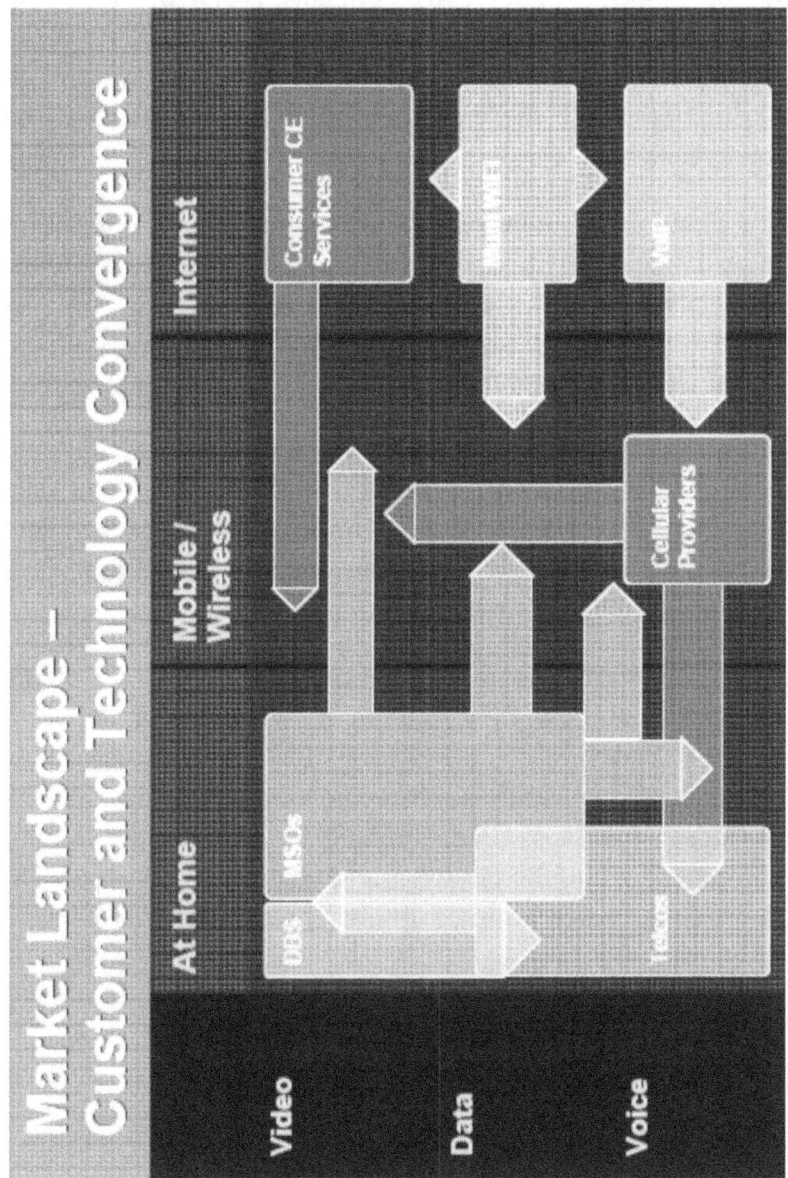

Figure 9: Technology convergence (Moloney, **2007**)

If you think: "I'm fine, my company is not in the Media Industry," think again. There is a chance you have been already thrown in a fight and you are not even aware of it. No matter where the epicenter is, this earthquake will be felt everywhere.

For example, a huge amount of money in the eletronics industry goes to "media players" like TVs, sound systems, DVD players, VCRs, etc. Will them survive? Probably this is not the right question. Probably the right question is: When will all of them be gone? [85]

Of course the fight is more intense in the media and communication industries, but it is not limited to them. The big change is related to how information is packed and distributed, and any company, in one way or another, deal with packing and distributing information.

Think about advertising. All companies right now are trying to figure out how they can build awareness in a world where advertising is considerably less mass driven. How can a company reach people who don't read newspapers anymore, spend less time watching TV – a lot more in their computers or mobile device – and when they do watch TV, they skip commercial interruptions through their TiVos?

---

[85] See more about this in chapters eight: "Mapping the Media Pipelines" and nine: "The Hypermedium"

SIX

The Crumbling Advertising Mold

There is a concealed deal in the old advertising model: consumers get subsidized news or entertainment in exchange for their attention at commercial breaks or to the printed advertisements. But this model breaks apart with the arrival of the digital medium. Consumers become less passive. Ad-avoidance rises. In this chapter we see how the old one-way, cluttered advertising model is giving way to a two-way pulled (and therefore more precise and less intrusive) model. In the old one-way pipeline, advertisers had no option than the very inefficient push strategy. In this chapter we see how the new digital pipeline and the new behaviors are opening up appealing alternatives. Even though advertisers are increasingly using the digital medium, many advertisers, stuck in the old paradigm, keep pushing one-way authoritative messages. Finally we take a look at some examples of ideas and experiments within the "hyper-oral society" mindset. We talk about the role of reputation and how it interplays with the ability of getting people's attention.

“How did Dog Fish Head find a customer like him? They didn't. He found them.

Eric Clemons, a professor at the Wharton School, is an aficionado of Dog Fish Head World Wide Imperial Stout beer at $160 per case. How did Dog Fish Head find a customer like him? They didn't. He found them. Clemons was not always a connoisseur of rare beers, but after trying Victory Hop Devil beer, the top ranked India Pale Ale at the time, he learned of Dog Fish Head, as well as Victory's Strom King Stout and other niche beers through the Internet. Clemons notes that he would never have bought the Dog Fish Head without the reviews on rarebeer.com and without the chain of experiences with ever-more interesting beers along the way.

See the paper "From Niches to Riches the Anatomy of the Long Tail" (Brynjolfsson, Hu, & Smith, 2006)

Let's get back to that mass production you've set up in chapter four. So, after setting up your factory, you are into mass-production mode and you want sell your product to the masses. But they need to know about your product. You need mass advertising.

You can try climbing on a box in a busy plaza and talk out loud about your product. If you have a good pitch some people will stop to listen to you. Most of the others will ignore you.

As you get more productive and your factory increases the output, you will need another strategy if you want reach thousands or millions of people.

So you think about printing flyers and distribute them on the street, or have them delivered to people's house. Now it is getting better. One flyer well designed, one mold, mass production of flyers, mass distribution.

But then you find out there is another company selling newspapers that deliver their newspapers to the same houses you want deliver your flyers. In fact, they can print your flyers for you or, even better, they can insert your message in the middle of their news.

Soon you are placing messages within newspapers, radio shows and TV programs. And you are getting outstanding results. Instead of selling to just a few hundred "people," now you are selling to millions of "consumers." [86]

By the middle of the twenty-first century, advertising placed in the middle of a popular TV show could get your message delivered to more than half of all households in the country.[87]

The model was working very well for all parts involved. The consumers could get information and entertainment for free – or at lower costs – because advertisers were paying a big part of Media company costs. Media companies could get an additional stream of revenue from advertisers. And advertisers could get their messages delivered to millions of consumers.

But to work well, this model requires typical mass consumers who passively watch, or hear, or read the one-way communication that comes to their senses.

The model breaks apart when consumers become active, when they take control, skipping advertising, switching

---

[86] Notice that at this point, "people" is replaced by a new concept: consumers. That's around the time when the specific is replaced by the average and the individual customer is replaced by the mass.

[87] Take a look at "List of most-watched television broadcasts" at Wikipedia.

channels, time-shifting with their DVRs,[88] picking – through the internet – the news they want to read, and favoring podcasts[89] against radio.

There was a concealed deal in the old model. Consumers could watch a TV show for free provided they watched passively the advertisements inserted in the middle of the show. Advertisers were paying for the show in exchange for consumers' attention at break time.

But now, such unspoken deal is at risk. In a study from University of Southern California Annenberg School's Center for the Digital Future, TV viewers were asked if they generally turn to do something else when TV commercials come on: *"... more than half said yes: 84% of Swedes, 66% among the Japanese and 69% among those from Singapore. A separate study of U.S. viewers found 90-95% engage in some ad avoidance behavior."* [90]

Now imagine you are in UK and you want people to know about your product. You know the audience for the Soccer World Cup will be huge. It costs you a good amount of money. But you believe it is well spent money, so you end up getting your advertising inserted at the break time. After the game, you see the ratings confirming the audience was huge. Mission accomplished, right? Maybe not.

---

[88] Time-shifting means recording TV (or radio) programs to watch them later at a more convenient time, usually skipping the commercial breaks. DVR stands for Digital Video Recording.

[89] Podcast refers to audio files (with news, blogs, radio programs, etc.) that people upload from the Internet into their music players (iPods, etc.) to listen when they want. See "Heard on the Street – Podcasting will change radio, not kill it." (Economist, 2006)

[90] See "Lifestyles of the Ad Averse," Millward Brown study, Feb'07 (MillwardBrown, 2007)

Maybe most of your intended audience was in the kitchen, making some tea, when your ad was showing at the TV in the family room.

In 1998, BBC published an article showing that the number of people turning to the kitchen at break time is so big that it requires thorough preparation to avoid problems in the UK power grid:[91]

> And one thing's for sure - at half-time, millions of people in the UK will heave themselves up from their sofas, amble into the kitchen and switch on the kettle for that great British pick-me-up - tea.
>
> This mass synchronized tea-break has in the past caused huge power surges and problems for the National Grid, which operates the high-voltage transmission network in England and Wales.

Ad avoidance is not new. People have been devising ways to skip advertising since the old times of radio.[92]

Device Shuts Off Radio Advertising; Tunes in Music

RADIO listeners who dislike advertising announcements and long speeches will welcome a new invention that automatically shuts off voice programs.

The device, known as the "radio advertising eliminator," will operate the radio only when musical programs are coming over the air. Just as soon as any voice announcement is made from the station, the radio receiver is turned off and is not turned on again until the musical program resumes.

The radio voice eliminator was invented by Dr. Gledson W. Kenrick, of Tufts College. It was demonstrated at the annual meeting of the American Association for the Advancement of Science. Of course, when the listener wants to listen to speeches or mixed programs, the device must be disconnected from the receiver.

It is believed that the new device uses a vibrating reed tuned to a predominant voice frequency to operate a relay which turns the set on and off.

This radio advertising eliminator will shut off any voice programs, but will turn on radio when the music starts.

Figure 10: Automatic Ad Skipping In 1934 (Vedrashko, 2007)

---

[91] See (Football trouble brewing for National Grid, 1998) at BBC.
[92] See this and other ad-avoidance related articles at the blog Advertising Lab.

For long time advertisers have talked about ad-avoidance but the concerns about it have been kept at bay.

But now such concerns are moving to the center stage as it is getting harder and harder to get people's attention; especially the younger generations.

The digital natives, raised in the world of video games and cluttered advertising, grew aware of the value of their attention and learned to focus on what mattered to them. Having at their hand multiple resources like laptops, mobile phones, instant messages and SMS, they learned to multitask and selectively drive their attention, discarding instinctively the irrelevant and intrusive advertising messages.

> The need to manage time efficiently is leading to a generation of "ad-avoiders," ready to shut out advertising inputs if it is not perceived as entertaining or informative. Two thirds of 16–24 year-olds in the UK indicate that they largely ignore TV ads. This compares to less than a quarter of those aged 65 or older. Respondents of a survey in the UK deemed skipping through ad-breaks at "30 times normal speed" as the most attractive feature of the PVR. [Personal Video Recorder, same as DVR]
>
> See "Digital Natives – How Is the Younger Generation Reshaping the Telecom and Media Landscape?"
> (Buvat, Mehra, & Braunschvig, 2007)

We can single out the three main factors driving the change:

1. *Advertising clutter is becoming unbearable. "TNS Media Intelligence has 2 million brands in its database and is adding an average of 700 per day. In 2003 alone, 26,893 new food and household products*

were introduced, including 115 deodorants, 187 breakfast cereals, and 303 women's fragrances, according to Mintel International Group Ltd.'s Global New Products Database." [93]

2. People can now easily skip ads. *"There is no doubt that technology will make it easier to skip commercials. The challenge for advertisers and broadcasters is to come out with more innovative solutions."* [94]

3. People behavior is changing from passive consumption to active control of their time and attention. They can now easily jump to competing mediums. *"More choice means that viewers can now focus only on what they want to see – more content and more channels are catering to their needs, but this does not necessarily translate to more time spent on TV as a medium. It will lead to more focused viewing."*[95]

There is still much debate going on about how long it will take for the Media landscape to actually change. How much relevant can become ad skipping? Will Internet ever replace TV broadcasting?

Some argue that if prime-time loses its meaning because more and more people time-shift with their DVRs, there will be still prime-content. Instead of peaks of audience at specific times of the day we will have peaks of audience for specific shows that will be watched by a big audience at the

---

[93] See "The Vanishing Mass Market," by Anthony Bianco, Business Week, Jul'04. (Bianco, 2004)

[94] See "The Death of Primetime?" (The Death of Primetime?, 2007)

[95] Ibid.

most convenient time for each person. *"...and the advertising aired during that content will still carry a premium."* [96]

Others see a crisis that will turn the advertising world upside down.

IBM has written in a 2007 study: *"The next 5 years will hold more change for the advertising industry than the previous 50 did. Increasingly empowered consumers, more self-reliant advertisers and ever-evolving technologies are redefining how advertising is sold, created, consumed and tracked."* [97]

Professor Stephen P.Bradley at Harvard Business School states, *"The reality for the advertising industry is that the old model is broken. The most effective advertising medium for decades has been television. But this traditional advertising [vehicle] is getting more expensive while also reaching fewer people. People may be watching more television hours, but their attention is spread across many more channels."* [98]

Accenture states in a 2007 study about the advertising industry: *"Change will be decisive, it will be rapid and it will transform the industry... ... Change is coming, and businesses will have to invest and change radically to get in or to stay in the game. But Accenture believes that the rewards will justify the effort. The long-term future of the*

[96] See "The Death of Primetime?" (The Death of Primetime?, 2007)

[97] See "The end of advertising as we know it," (Berman, Battino, Shipnuck, & Neus, 2007)

[98] See "Broadband: Remaking the Advertising Industry" by Julia Hanna at HBS Working Knowledge, Sep'07 (Hanna, 2007)

advertising business — if we will even be calling it that a decade from now — is bright." [99]

In October 2008, Tom Rogers, TiVo president and founder of CNBC, warned attendees at the Association of National Advertisers Conference: "*In the next two to three years the television industry is going to face an advertising crisis more severe than our financial crisis.*" He suggests that people will have no excuses for not realizing this crisis is approaching: "*You have sufficient warning about television commercial avoidance and the growing epidemic of fast forwarding thru ads. Look what happened to the music business. Look what is happening to the newspaper business. If you don't come out of this room acting urgently, what's going to happen in the television business will probably make that look like kids' stuff. If you think this recession is tough to deal with, believe me it is nothing compared to the downturn in your brands that will come if you do nothing while television advertising goes avoided.*"[100]

Where unimaginative people see a big trouble, creative ones see a big opportunity. While some will miss the old mass campaigns that could reach a huge number of households sticking a message in the whole country's brain, others will realize those reach levels are part of the old mass-market paradigm. In this new world, they don't need that anymore. Now they have available a two-way pipe. Now they have a feedback loop. Now they can be less

---

[99] See "Facing the digital reality: the path to future high performance in advertising" at Accenture web site. (Accenture, 2007)

[100] See "TV Industry Faces Ad Avoidance Crisis More Severe than Financial Crisis, Warns TiVo CEO" by Jack Meyers at The Huffington Post, Oct'08 (Myers, 2008)

intrusive, just teasing and provoking until people engage in an instructive conversation about how the advertiser can help them solve their problems or make their life better. Now the advertiser can be more precise and avoid wasting money by pushing messages on "consumers" that were not interested at all in their solutions.

> " Advertisers scream their message to millions of people so just a few that need their product can hear them.

The mass advertising model is very inefficient to most products. Advertisers scream their message to millions of people so just a few who need their product can hear them. How many advertisements have you seen of products that have nothing to do with you? Young people watching ads of geriatric products. Elder people watching ads for cool stuff for teenagers. Teenagers watching adds of disposable diapers. Men watching ads for feminine products.

Of course, the advertisers try to select the shows whose audience better match the people to whom they want pass their message. But even taking such care just a small percentage of all the people reached is affected by the message. *"Even an optimistic response rate is less than one percent of viewers."* [101] For the other 99% the message is noise. And for advertisers this noise is wasted money. Advertisers would prefer not to pay for all of those ineffective pitches. At the same time all those other people would prefer not to hear all that noise. But in the one-way pipe there is not much that can be done. And as more and more companies decide to scream through the pipe, just to

---

[101] See "Facing the digital reality: the path to future high performance in advertising" (Accenture, 2007)

affect a small percentage of consumers at the other end, they clutter the advertising space and the noise becomes unbearable. If given a chance, people tune out and the whole system efficiency becomes even worse.

Someone could argue that beyond the short term response rate to an advertisement there is also a cumulative effect that will result in future sales. Repetition will eventually generate familiarity and therefore a favorable attitude. Some studies suggest that even the not consciously noticed stimulus have a subliminal effect enhancing *"a person's feelings towards what's otherwise a neutral object."* [102] This proposition can be true but it highlights another issue with the mass advertising model: Advertisers "do not really know whether it is working or not. Traditional advertising requires an expensive act of faith by its buyers because the linkage between the broadcast of an ad and a consumer buying decision is unclear and uncertain." [103]

· · ·

So, what do you do about your advertising plans? Should you keep pushing your messages through the traditional media pipes even though you know people are increasingly blocking or filtering out your ads?

The good news is that we still have time to learn. The old advertising model won't die abruptly. It will take some time until the new digital medium takes over; until broadband

---

[102] See "Banner Work Even When Over looked" at Advertising Lab. (Vedarshko, 2007)

[103] See "Facing the digital reality: the path to future high performance in advertising" (Accenture, 2007)

and all those new digital resources – the gadgets and the services – get distributed to the majority of world's people. But the push model is getting old and weak.

The bad news is that – for the same reason above – we still need to scream our message in the old wasteful ineffective one-way pipe.

But advertisers are already trying new approaches.

One current trend is the replacement of so-called mass communication by targeted segmented communication: narrowcast, instead of broadcast; micromarketing, instead of mass marketing. The proliferation of TV channels, radio channels, specialized magazines and mobile devices give advertisers an opportunity to be more precise in attempting to reach their specific niche of consumers. This also makes the message more relevant to the audience, decreasing the odds of ad-avoidance behavior.

> "Mass is still mass, but we're nearing the tipping point," says Robin Kent, chairman and CEO of Universal McCann, a media buying agency. "Then there will be huge segmentation."
>
> See "The Vanishing Mass Market" by Anthony Bianco, Business Week, Jul'04 (Bianco, 2004)

Online advertising plays a critical role in a micromarketing strategy allowing advertisers to become very specific on whom they want reach. It also allows higher efficacy of the money spent because the two-way pipe allows the advertiser to know how many consumers responded to the message and therefore pay just for those ones.

Leading advertisers are already shifting their advertising spending towards online media.

"Online is getting to the point where it may be more important than the 30-second TV spot," said Joel Ewanick, VP of Marketing for Hyundai MotorAmerica.[104]

However, moving to online advertising does not necessarily protect advertisers from ad-avoidance.

In an online survey conducted in March 2008, 73% of respondents said advertisements are extremely annoying. But the online advertisements, which we could expect to be better targeted and more relevant, don't solve the issue. In fact they get a worse evaluation: *"48% of respondents say the Internet has the most invasive or irritating advertisements, exceeding 27% picking TV."* [105]

So, prisoners of the old one-way-push paradigm or limited by the still dominant and antiquated one-way pipe, advertisers try to sneak-in under peoples' ad-avoidance radar.

One way to accomplish that is through product placement. Put the product within the program itself, instead of having stand-alone ad insertions at break-time. Such strategy can go from a simple appearance of the refrigerator brand, or the cereal box brand, in the background of a kitchen scene, to having the product in the foreground as an active

---

[104] See "General Motors to Spend $1.5 Billion on Online Advertising" by Janet Meyners, Mar'08 at Pilgrim Marketing blog.   (Meiners, 2008)

[105] See "You Can't Avoid Ad Avoidance" by Greg Stuart, Sep'08 at AdWeek.com (Stuart, 2008) or read the complete survey: (Stuart & Vizu, Why Consumers Hate Advertising & What They Are Doing About It, 2008)

participant of the program, as part of the storyline. *"The possibilities for an expanded presence for product placements have spawned a cottage industry of firms that specialize in brokering such placements... some placement brokers are becoming so sophisticated that they get input from producers, writers and advertisers as to how their client's product could be integrated into a script in a creative way."*[106]

One discussion around product placements is about how intrusive it should be. *"The industry thinking seems to be that more intrusiveness equates more effectiveness."* [107] Advertisers want the product to be noticed. But too much intrusiveness can disrupt the program, irritate consumers and lead them to raise their defenses.

Another way to try to beat people's ad-avoidance are sponsorships, celebrity endorsements, superimposing logos and messages within programs – like a Nike logo showing at the corner of the TV screen during a soccer match – and increasing investments in alternative media, like cinema, – where people can't use their mobile devices – bus interiors, ski chairlifts, and others.

If there is a good fit, if the product placement goes well within the storyline, if the sponsorship or the endorsement presents good synergy with the message, such approaches can work. But the basic idea is still stuck in the old paradigm of mass media. It is still trying to force the message, to push it, within people's lives.

---

[106] See "The Future of Television Advertising" in Marketing Communication: Emerging Trends and Developments p.113-132, (Lowrey, Shrum, & McCarty, 2005)
[107] Ibid.

In February 2008, an article was posted in TheMediaOnline blog with the title: "Beating the ad-avoidance radar." The article states the escalating issue of ad-avoidance before asking: *"So if you are an advertiser, how do you make sure consumers don't avoid your ad and that your message is the one remembered ahead of the other 2,999 ads seen on a daily basis?"* The author writes: *"The answer is simple – you need to slip in under people's built-in ad-avoidance radar. How? By being smarter, more inventive and more collaborative. Your brand needs to become a part of the editorial environment, facilitate conversations and stop interrupting people's already busy lives."* [108]

A reader posted his reaction to the article: *"There is something slightly horrifying about this article. Just the notion that advertisers are spending their energy trying to figure out how to beat our desire not to interact with them, and that, by contrast, the majority of people are desperately trying not to be advertised at, points to a deep problem. It seems like it's about time that advertisers realize that people don't want to be bothered by them. Not directly, not sneakily, not at all. Businesses need to come to grips with a world in which unwanted information can, and will, be aggressively filtered out. And understand a completely new marketing paradigm which is based on something other than forcing your message down people's eyes or ears."* [109]

That's the difference between the old mass advertising school and the new one that is rising. While the old one is trying to *"slip in under people's built-in ad-avoidance radar"* – trying to push a message in – the new one is trying

---

[108] See "Beating the ad-avoidance radar" by Richard Lord, Feb'08 at
   MediaOnline Blog (Lord, 2008)
[109] Ibid. Within the comments section.

to learn how to earn the right to be included in people's social radar [110] – and therefore to have the message pulled into a two-way conversation.

> ❝ In the new villages the people are the ones deciding who gets in or out of their radar screen.

As people move back to the villages,[111] – led by digital natives – the behaviors and way of thinking are changing. TV broadcasting monologues are losing ground to dynamic interactive conversations. People now can avoid becoming hostages of the ad clutter with its widespread screaming. They don't need to surrender to the old advertising push model anymore, because there is a new competing medium that allow people to pull, to close the loop, to participate, to engage in real time conversations, building communities, abandoning the lonely individual abstraction and taking back the control.

In the new villages, the people own the point of view. They are the ones deciding who deserves their attention; who gets in or out of their radar screen.

In the new villages, Media companies will need to find a way to keep intermediating the "attention market" or they will need to increase the price of their services to cover the costs that have been funded by the advertisers.

And as the dominant medium and the world change, advertisers also need to change. Instead of broadcasting a one-size-fits-all one-way message to "consumers,"

---

[110] See at the Preface of this book how people are leveraging the digital medium to set up a social radar where they keep refreshing the links in their social network and monitoring its flow of information.

[111] See chapter 3: Back to the Village

advertisers will do better inserting themselves, legitimately, within those "people" conversations – keeping in mind they are active people; no longer the passive consumers at the recipient end of the whole supply chain. Instead of pushing information down the consumers' throats, as they had to do in the past when the information pipes allowed just the one-way pushed flow, now they need to elicit participative discussions.

Instead of thinking on reach, advertisers should focus on how to be easily reached; on how to clean the path and spread the word so people can find them.

Advertisers need to become a *"good guest, not a gate-crasher by creating both pull and pass-along tactics that afford rejecters the ability to invite marketers into their personal space and that of their network."* [112]

This is what Miller Lite tried to do in their 2006 "Man Laws" campaign:[113]

> The campaign asked consumers to catch their friends, co-workers, or people on the street violating a Man Law. They were asked to take a picture of the violation and send it to a website built to display all of these pictures and develop a dialogue. Once pictures were on the website, consumers were asked to vote on their favorite submission, which was then featured in FHM [US men's magazine] the following month.

---

[112] See "Lifestyles of the Ad Averse," (MillwardBrown, 2007)
[113] Ibid.

This campaign is a good illustration of how to reach and engage Ad Avoiders because it touches on all four tenets mentioned above.[see the study]

1. The campaign provides conversational currency and entertainment value
2. It allows consumers to join in the campaign
3. It uses various media synergistically
4. It encourages as well as provides valued content for pass-along

That campaign became wildly popular, generating a strong media buzz, hundreds of thousands of entries to an online site, and pop-culture references. It cut through the advertising clutter and put Miller Lite within people's radar. However, it failed to help increase the beer sales. Probably because it didn't give people a reason why they should drink Miller Lite. As consequence the campaign was put out of the air by Jan of 2007.[114]

Another company that has been trying to find its way in this new environment is Procter & Gamble. In a market test with the dish detergent Dawn, the company was able to increase its volume by more than 90%, working with a network of moms who spread the company's message within their own social networks.

P&G established its own in-house word-of-mouth agency, which claims to have *"the nation's largest legion of connectors"* – 225,000 teens in their "Tremor" network and 600,000 moms in their Vocalpoint network by 2006.[115]

---

[114] See "Man Laws benched" by Tom Daykin at JS Online, Jan'07
[115] See "I Sold It Through the Grapevine," Business Week, May'06
(Berner, 2006)

They explain the term connectors in their site: [Connectors] *"are not your average consumer. Our connectors have social networks 5 to 6 times larger than normal. Connectors have a propensity to talk, are highly influential, and amplify YOUR product's message across their networks of friends, family, co-workers and acquaintances."* [116]

> **How far can a company go trying to insert itself in people's radar before jeopardizing the company's reputation and people's friendships?**

P & G initiative has generated some controversy because it does not require its connectors to disclose their affiliation with the company. P&G position is that the company puts its connectors fully in charge of what they want to tell their friends: *"you don't tell the consumer what to say."* Others disagree mentioning the danger of having *"friends treating one another as advertising pawns, undercutting social trust."* [117] Some connector moms come to P&G defense: "We are just moms doing what all mothers have been doing for years - helping our friends by offering our opinions on the products we try, and passing along coupons we're not going to use to help others save." [118]

This is a new world. It will take time until advertisers can really understand where the line is. How far can a company go, trying to insert itself in people's radar before jeopardizing the company's reputation and people's friendships?

---

[116] See the **P&G Word of Mouth Marketing** page.
[117] See "**I Sold It Through the Grapevine**," (Berner, 2006)
[118] Ibid. (in the comments section – posted on May 19, 2006 9:39 PM)

At the villages your reputation is fundamental. It defines your ability to buy or sell and your ability to keep friendships.

> **People understand the value of their attention because they are conscious of its scarcity.**

The attention that you will be able to capture depends on your reputation and on the relevance of what you have to say. Once you get elected to be within people's social radar, people will follow you. And any participation you have in the conversation, anything you say, anything you do, the quality of your products or your comments, will affect your reputation. Higher reputation brings higher visibility and more attention. You can make it grow or you can damage it until you get thrown out of the people's social radar.

At the villages, reputations are built bottom up, based on your actions or comments and on what is said through the grapevine. You cannot build them through top-down pitches anymore, because people are not any longer sitting passively absorbing the messages coming through the tube. At the villages people are actively driving their attention to what they believe is worth of it.

If there is still an opportunity to trade people's attention for advertisers' sales pitch, – like giving a coupon so people pay attention to your message – this trade will not go undercover anymore. It won't be a mass deal. It will be a one-on-one negotiation where people understand the value of their attention because they are conscious of its scarcity. And even if you buy attention, what people hear from you will not be taken for granted. It will be checked through their network and it will have an impact on your reputation, for good or for bad. As a consequence it will affect the chances you will have in the future to get further attention or sell your products or services.

. . .

See below part of the table from chapter three (Back to the Village) related to the changes we face as we move to a hyper-oral society:[119]

Literate Societies		Hyper-Oral Societies
Feeling of Closure	vs.	Back to Conversation
Boxed Content	vs.	Ever changing experience
Authorial authority	vs.	Collective Creation
Lonely Reader	vs.	Online Communities
Individual Abstraction	vs.	Participatory Panopticon
Analytical, Linear and Hierarchical thought	vs.	Aggregative, Parallel, Networked thought
Investigative and Conciliatory	vs.	Engagement

Table 3: from Literate to Hyper-Oral Societies

---

[119] See chapter three – "Back to the Village"

Digital natives are already developing shopping habits very different from the ones of the older generations:[120]

…Using Google and a variety of online shopping sites, Mary researched dresses online, getting a sense for what styles she liked and reading information about what was considered stylish that year. Next, Mary and her friends went to the local department store as a small group, toting along their digital cameras (even though they're banned). They tried on the dresses, taking pictures of each other in the ones that fit. Upon returning home, Mary uploaded the photos to her Facebook and asked her broader group of friends to comment on which they liked the best. Based on this feedback, she decided which dress to purchase, but didn't tell anyone because she wanted her choice to be a surprise. Rather than returning to the store, Mary purchased the same dress online at a cheaper price based on the information on the tag that she had written down when she initially saw the dress. She went for the cheaper option because her mother had given her a set budget for homecoming shopping; this allowed her to spend the rest on accessories.

In the 1980s, Alan Kay declared that, "technology is anything that wasn't around when you were born." In other words, what is perceived as technology to adults is often ubiquitous if not invisible to youth. In telling this story, Mary's mother was perplexed by the technology choices made by her daughter. Yet, most likely, Mary saw her steps in a practical way: research, test out, get feedback, purchase. Her choices were to maximize her options, make a choice that would be socially accepted, and purchase the dress at the cheapest price. Her steps were not about maximizing technology, but about using it to optimize what she did care about.

---

[120] See "Technology and the World of Consumption" at Digital Youth Research web site. (Boyd, 2008)

SEVEN

A Scale-Free World, For Good or For Bad?

What would be the cost of most of the things we have today if they were all handmade and designed specifically for each one of us? How much would we know today if books could only be copied by hand? How would have Edison created the light-bulb if he didn't have access to the basic knowledge of electricity? The mold concept improved productivity, allowed widespread distribution of books and extended our memory, but we lost the speed and fluidity of the live debates. It allowed high output but it imposed uniformity and killed individuality. Now, the digital medium is allowing us to break the mold while keeping the gains and getting back what we have lost. This means we must release our thoughts from average thinking. We need to learn about the scale-free nature of the World Wide Web with its power laws and counterintuitive characteristics. In this chapter we discuss how we are moving from a Gaussian world to a scale-free world. Then we take a look at different perspectives on what is about to come, for good or for bad.

The wonderful progress of the present century is, in a very great degree, due to the invention and improvement of the steam engine, and to the ingenious application of its power to kinds of work that formerly taxed the physical energies of the human race. [121]

After James Watt's patent was granted in 1769, steam engines spread across the Western world powering factories, mills, pumps, ships and trains. For that patent James Watt is considered the father of the steam engine.

Steam power triggered and fed the Industrial Revolution – also called, for this reason, "The Age of Steam" – leading to an extraordinary increase in production per capita and changing dramatically the world after the eighteenth century.

However, Watt's ideas just came to life as he worked on repairing a previous version of a steam engine, which was invented by Thomas Newcomen 57 years before, in 1712.[122] Newcomen's engine, in turn, was basically an improvement on Thomas Savery's engine – patented in 1698 – which was based on Dennis Papin's Digester or pressure cooker of 1679 – 90 years before Watt's engine.

So, despite the important role played by James Watt's patent in the steam engine history, he didn't come out with it alone. The myth of the lonely genius is something relatively new, created in the modern literate society, rooted in its authorial authority.[123] James Burke challenged such myth. He defended the idea that scientific discoveries and

---

[121] See quote from R.H.Thurston's book: "A History of the Growth of the Steam Engine" at "The Steam Engine" page at University of Dayton. (Bolon, 2001)

[122] Read more about it in "Dreams of Steam: A History of Steam Power" at the Museum of American Heritage site (MOAH, 2005) and in "The History of Steam Engines" at About.com (Bellis)

[123] See chapter two: "Changing Media, Changing Us"

technological advances materialize trough a process that involves an interconnected "web" of knowledge, people, and events. In his book "Connections" (from 1978!) he wrote:

> Two points arise from this way of looking at the process of change and innovation. One is that, as we have seen, no inventor works alone. The myth of the lonely genius, filled with vision and driven to exhaustion by his dream, may have been deliberately fostered by Edison, but even he did not invent without help from his colleagues and predecessors…
>
> The second point is that the ease with which information can be spread is critical to the rate at which change occurs. The inventive output of Western technology can be said to have occurred in three major surges. The first – the Medieval Industrial Revolution – came after the establishment of safe lines of communication between the communities of Europe, as order was re-established in the wake of the invasions of the tenth century. The second occurred in the seventeenth century when the scientific community began to make use of printing to exchange ideas on a major scale. The third followed the nineteenth century development of telecommunications.
>
> See the book "Connections", by J.Burke, 1978, p.291.
> (Burke, Connections, 1978)

At prehistoric times we were hunter-gatherers and had little spare time to do anything else than search for food and fulfill our basic human needs.

Over time we've learned how to produce food. We've learned to build a few tools, cultivate plants and domesticate a few animals to help us with our tasks. At that point, with the help of the animals and more efficient usage of our energy to get food, we gained extra time.

With that additional time we could then build better tools and think on more productive ways to do what we had to do, therefore getting even more spare time feeding a virtuous cycle.[124]

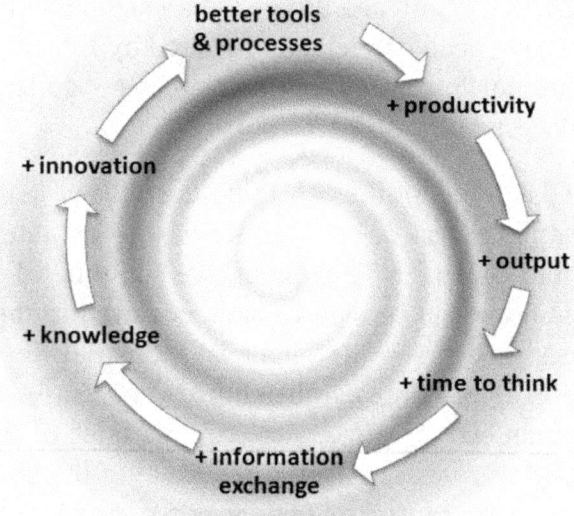

Figure 11: innovation/productivity virtuous cycle

But the amount of knowledge we could handle was limited by our memory and by the number of people that could be reached by voice or direct apprenticeship. So, new technologies and ideas often vanished with their creators, or they stayed enclosed within one village or group never reaching another group that could make a good use of it;

---

[124] Two very good books on this topic are: "Guns, Germs and Steel: The Fates of Human Societies" by Jared Diamond (Diamond, 2005) and "Understanding the Process of Economic Change" by Douglass C. North. (North, 2005)

another group that could extend the technology's life in case the original group disappeared, or even develop that technology into additional inventions further improving productivity.

125

The Mayas and Aztecs from Pre-Columbian Mexico would have developed in a different direction and probably would have become even more powerful societies if they had big domestic animals to help them with their tasks – like the ones the Europeans had.

Not far away, the Incas in Peru had the llamas, but they didn't have corn what would be an opportune enrichment to their diet.

It took more than five thousand years until the llamas could meet the corn; despite they were as close as roughly 300 walking-days apart.

When we developed the writing technology we extended our memory and reach. Writing technology triggered further innovation and higher productivity but it remained, for many centuries, a privilege of very few people. So, its reach was still very limited as well as its permanence. Very few copies existed of original texts. Just a few people had access to them and many ideas and concepts were lost when those texts were destroyed for one reason or another.

When we came out with the printing press technology, permanence and reach changed dramatically. It allowed the production of a massive number of copies at very low cost.

---

[125] Walking 300 days, 8 hours a day at 1 mile per hour would cover 2,400 miles, a lot more than needed to go from the Inca empire to the Aztec empire. This is a hypothetical example inspired by "Guns, Germs and Steel: The Fates of Human Societies" by Jared Diamond, (Diamond, 2005) where he shows how knowledge diffusion and geographies affected the fate of different societies.

Having many copies, it was easier to spread the information and to protect it from disappearance if the original work was eventually destroyed.

Printing made it easier to accumulate knowledge and to expand it, so people could develop new and more complex concepts, founded on the more basic ones. The stock of human knowledge gained a steady, long-range, escalation mechanism. Instead of local bursts followed by fading, the human knowledge became distributed and accumulated through time, cross-geographies, reaching more people. Such cumulative knowledge was then applied to cumulative improvements of technologies and production processes increasing exponentially overall output.

Printing was the precursor of the mass manufacturing equation:[126] one design; one mold; many replicas through mass production; mass awareness through mass advertising; mass distribution.

Once we figured out this equation and spread the concept (through printed material), once we built a mold and put it to work, all we had to do was to control the machine; feed it with supplies and distribute its output. Such a high level of output, allowed people to spend more time thinking. We could come out with the steam engine, and all the other engines that followed it, moving the machine even faster, increasing further the machine output. Food and basic needs weren't any longer the only issues we had time to bear in mind. Society could afford having an army of specialized thinkers.

---

[126] See chapter four: The Print Mold and the Mass Media Era.

Those thinkers worked on improving the standards and making the processes even more productive. Consequently we ended up having fantastic machines and processes working for us, improving exponentially society average wealth, from food production to medicine, from transportation to entertainment.

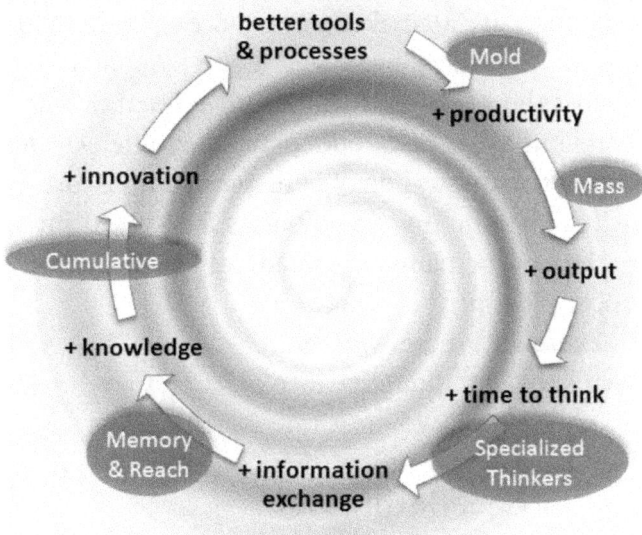

Figure 12: mass production powered the innovation/productivity virtuous cycle

The cost of production and distribution went down sharply, to a point where people now could own books and music, and could watch performances (on TV), which they would never be able to afford in the old days of the old villages.

The mold idea – the mass manufacturing – was a breakthrough that made those fantastic machines efficient and productive. The mold concept is what made them possible. It was applied with outstanding success to physical goods and information goods. So, people got more of both. But there were in both cases, some significant drawbacks.

Once the mold concept was applied to produce information goods, it altered how people dealt with information in the old villages. As we moved from village-style conversations to mass broadcasting, the information became more homogeneous. It also became more rigid. After all, information became a packaged good coughed out by a mold. It lost the speed and fluidity of a local debate where arguments built up fast, one over the other. It lost the dynamism of a discussion where propositions are refuted right away and solutions come out as a result of interaction among the participants. Instead of such participative experience, learning became a solitary exercise where we read static snapshots of thoughts in a printed book. And we are fine with that, because we know that without encapsulating the information goods within the mold, the massive distribution and the consequent build up of knowledge that we saw during the last few centuries couldn't have taken place.

> "Information became a packaged good coughed out by a mold.

On the other hand, once the mold concept was applied to produce physical goods, it also moved us into a more homogeneous world; a world of averages. We stopped producing a specific product for each person. Instead, now we do consumer research. We plot the results in normal distributions. We find out what are the things most of consumers want – the color, the shape, the size, the music tracks, the articles – so we can build a mold to satisfy the average consumer within our target audience. Of course the result we get is merely an average. Probably no consumer will get everything he or she wanted, but they can get something close. And they will be fine with that, because they understand things can become really expensive if they want to get something out of the mold, a product especially made to order, which would satisfy all their specific needs.

So the literate-mass-media era became the era when we built molds for everything; from thoughts to clothes to consumer electronics to management processes. Then, using the mold, we made thousands or millions of replicas of the original design and distributed them to the masses. This way people gained access to things they would never have if we were still building those things one by one. And because they were not built one by one, they were built to the average person, to the average-consumer. The literate-mass-media era became the era of static snapshots of normal distributions, the era of the average.

> "The literate-mass-media era became the era of the average.

In order to become more productive, we've learned to think in term of molds and averages, standard deviations and typical results. That's because we have to build a mold in order to mass-produce, and in order to build a mold we need to define its size. Therefore we pick the average size and aim at it. And once we get used to follow this thinking process, we then try to fit anything within the bell-shaped curve, focusing on its peak and discarding anything significantly different from the average.

Most research within organizations talks about typical results, standard deviation, levels of confidence; all concepts associated with the bell shaped Gaussian-mold reasoning.

Even when we realized a good amount of people or events could be far from the average we reacted by defining segments and one more time forcing the bell-shaped curve over those segments; building a specific mold for them.

> But it is not just social scientists who fall prey to this temptation to adopt a Gaussian view of the world. Business executives also are drawn to a Gaussian world. At one level it is much simpler – there is a meaningful "average consumer" that can be used to scale products and operations around – and it is a much more predictable world. In many respects, the history of Western business in the twentieth century represents an effort to build scalable operations through standardization designed to serve "average consumers."
>
> See "The Power of Power Laws" by John Hagel
> at his blog Edge Perspectives. (Hagel, 2007)

A Gaussian curve or a "normal" [127] distribution – works very well on helping us understand and deal with many sets of data, especially in natural science, where data points are frequently independent.

For example, we do not need to measure all men in US to learn most men's height in this country is around 5'9 and very few above 7'0. We simply need a representative sample so we can look to the normal distribution and its standard deviation extrapolating its results to the total population. We will find out that we have around 34 million

---

[127] The name "normal" reflects the prevalence we give in our thoughts to this kind of distribution.

men within 5'9" to 6'0" range of height and therefore plan
our production accordingly – could be shirts or pants or
space between seats in an airplane or anything else related
to height. We also consider that the number of people with
heights beyond a few sigma [128] deviation from the average
is insignificant.

Height Range	S.D.	Expected number
4'6" - 4'9"	-4σ	3200
4'9" - 5'0"	-3σ	135000
5'0" - 5'3"	-2σ	2100000
5'3" - 5'6"	-1σ	13600000
5'6" - 5'9"	average	34000000
5'9" - 6'0"	average	34000000
6'0" - 6'3"	1σ	13600000
6'3" - 6'6"	2σ	2100000
6'6" - 6'9"	3σ	135000
6'9" - 7'0"	4σ	3200
7'0" - 7'3"	5σ	28
7'3" - 7'6"	6σ	0

Table 4: Men's height distribution in U.S.   [129]

Gaussian curves are very popular in industrial sets. They
gave origin to the popular six sigma programs which refer
to the ability of manufacturing processes to keep production
within the mold, very close to the norm, with very little

---

[128] In this example less than 7,000 thousand men in almost 100 million
are beyond 3 sigma deviation (taller than 6'9" or shorter than 4'9").
This is less than 0.01%, therefore safe to discard. (from the mass
producer perspective – unfortunately for the outliers)

[129] See Statistics "Average and Standard Deviation" by Mark Lawrence
(Lawrence, 2005)

variation, very few defects – less than 3.4 products out of specification in 1 million opportunities.

But now we are learning that while the molds and averages, with their bell-shaped curves and standard deviation, work very well to some set of events, for many others they are completely inadequate and can lead to totally flawed reasoning.

Barabazi, from University of Notre Dame, and Bonabeau, chief scientist at Icosystem, described their experience when they first tried to map the Internet:

> When we began to map the Web, we expected the nodes to follow a bell-shaped distribution, as do people's heights. Instead we discovered certain nodes that defied explanation, almost as if we had stumbled on a significant number of people who were 100 feet tall, thus prompting us to coin the term "scale-free…" Over the past several years, researchers have uncovered scale-free structures in a stunning range of systems.
>
> See "Scale-Free Networks" at Scientific American
> (Barabasi & Bonabeau, 2003)

Scale-free networks lead to another kind of distribution, which are very different from the overused bell-shaped "normal" Gaussian curves. They lead to power law curves. While most results in a Gaussian curve are similar to the average with very few significantly different, in a power law, most results are very different from the average. Power law curves don't have a flat top. Therefore they don't have typical events, their averages have no meaning, and their variances tend to infinite (see figure in the next page).

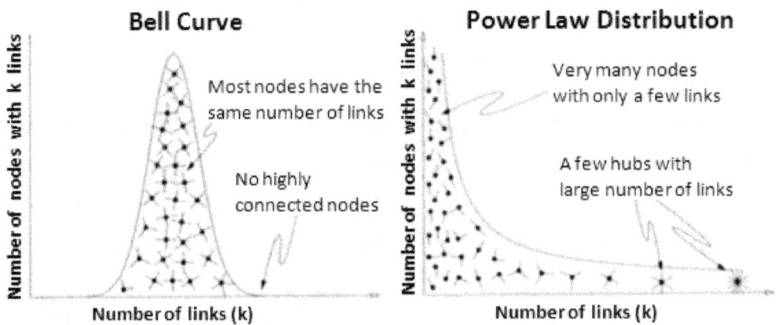

Figure 13: Random and Scale-Free Network Distributions. Adapted from "Linked: The New Science of Networks", by A.Barabasi (Barabasi, Linked: the new science of networks, 2003)

While in a Gaussian world it is totally safe to focus on the average and discard the atypical events beyond a few sigma deviation, in the Scale-free world the outliers have more meaning and greater consequences than anything in the middle.

Andriani, from Duham Business School, and McKelvey, from UCLA School of management, point out: *"In a 'normal' world, where distributions show finite variance, extreme events are so different from the typical and so rare that they don't significantly influence either the mean or the variance. Hence, ignoring them is a safe strategy."*... *"A power law world is dominated by extreme events ignored in a Gaussian-world. In fact, the fat tails*[130] *of power law*

---

[130] Be careful when you see references to the "tail" of the curve because in some instances, despite addressing the same subject, the chart presented is not of the power law distribution and has different axes. The "tail" ends up having the opposite meaning. Read more about these different ways to plot the curve on: "Zipf, Power-laws, and Pareto" by L. A. Adamic, Oct'00. (Adamic, 2000)

distributions make large extreme events orders-of-magnitude more likely." [131]

In power law distributions concentration is the norm. A few hold the most while thousands of others get little. In power law distributions most of the data points are far below average. Scale-free worlds are not egalitarian at all.

We are so used to bell curve distributions that power law distributions can seem odd.

> ...we know that power law distributions tend to arise in social systems where many people express their preferences among many options. We also know that as the number of options rise, the curve becomes more extreme. This is a counter-intuitive finding - most of us would expect a rising number of choices to flatten the curve, but in fact, increasing the size of the system increases the gap between the #1 spot and the median spot.
>
> See "Power Laws, Weblogs, and Inequality," Feb'03 in Clay Shirky's blog. (Shirky, 2003)

As the number of pages grows in the Internet we would expect that the additional pages should grab some share of the top ones leading us to a more egalitarian world. But what happens is that every time new people, or new pages, or new routers, get into the network they have to decide where to connect. The choice is not made randomly – what would give origin to a bell-shaped curve – but rather influenced by the topology that is already in place. New

---

[131] See "Beyond Gaussian Averages: Redirecting Management Research Toward Extreme Events and Power Laws" by Pierpaolo Andriani, Bill McKelvey, Jul'06. (Andriani & McKelvey, 2006)

entrants attach more often to more connected people, or pages, because they are most known and easier to find.

> By simply linking to those nodes, people exercise and reinforce a bias toward them... These two mechanisms – growth and preferential attachment – help to explain the existence of hubs: as new nodes appear, they tend to connect to the more connected sites, and these popular locations thus acquire more links over time than their less connected neighbors. And this "rich get richer" process will generally favor the early nodes, which are more likely to eventually become hubs.[132]
>
> See "Scale-Free Networks"
> (Barabasi & Bonabeau, Scale-Free Networks, 2003)

This "rich get richer" process is what has triggered a golden rush in the early stages of the Internet with big bets being placed on the most prominent hubs because they have higher probability to get even bigger.

So, considering this "rich get richer" process: Will one company at some point be able to fully dominate the Internet? (Some would say Google is on its way to do that.[133])

Barabasi and Bonabeau pointed out – using their model – a situation where the system can move from "rich-gets-richer" to "winner-takes-all" scenario and the network morphs from scale-free to star topology, which has the

---

[132] Hubs are highly connected nodes. They are points of convergence in the network, reducing the number of steps between nodes. Airline routes, for example, make use of hubs in order to reduce the number of connections required in a flight from one small city to another.

[133] See "Winner-Take-All: Google and the Third Age of Computing" by Rich Skrenta, Jan'07 at Skrenta.com (Skrenta, 2007)

dominant player at the center with all other nodes linked to it:

> Interestingly, the mechanism of preferential attachment tends to be linear. In other words, a new node is twice as likely to link to an existing node that has twice as many connections as its neighbor. Redner and his colleagues at Boston University and elsewhere have investigated different types of preferential attachment and have learned that if the mechanism is faster than linear (for example, a new node is four times as likely to link to an existing node that has twice as many connections), one hub will tend to run away with the lion's share of connections. In such "winner take all" scenarios, the network eventually assumes a star topology with a central hub.
>
> See "Scale-Free Networks"
> (Barabasi & Bonabeau, Scale-Free Networks, 2003)

Ironically, such star topology – "winner-takes-all" – scenario would take us closer to an egalitarian world than any scale-free network would be able to do, because it portrays a world where everyone – except the central hub – is at the same level and just one degree apart. This is very close to the communist "perfect-world" ideal where everyone is at the same level, linked to a central government.

But such star topology model is rather unstable. Any failure in the central hub breaks the whole network apart leading the network to a different topology as M.Rosvall points out in his paper: "Complex Networks and Dynamics of an Information Network Model:" [134]

---

[134] See "Complex Networks and Dynamics of an Information Network Model," M.Rosvall, Feb'03, Univ. of Umea, Sweden. (Rosvall, 2003)

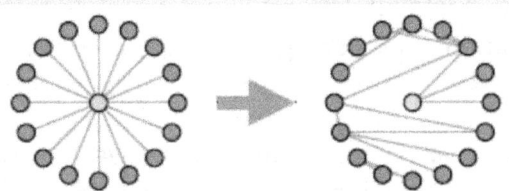

Figure 14: From perfect world to scale-free due to the destabilization of the central hub. (Rosvall, 2003)

In a perfect world, a single vertex that can differentiate all exit edges from each other might distribute all tasks and information efficiently (left panel). In real world networks, no perfect "distributor" exists because when each agent attempts to minimize the distances to all other agents, agents tend to be connected through more than one intermediate. Imperfections destabilize the central hub, and the agents in the network obtain a wide range of connectivity (right panel).

Because Napster – the once very popular music sharing site – operated in a star topology,[135] it was easy for the recording industry to shut it down.

"Having learned from Napster's troubles, current peer-to-peer networks tend to be decentralized. That is, nodes connect directly to one another rather than to a central server." [136]

So, instead of scale-free networks morphing into star topology it is more probable that star topologies would disintegrate into scale-free networks, as people would add

---

[135] The users should report which files they were sharing to Napster's central server. They also should query the central server to locate other users who had the files they were looking for.

[136] See "Zipf's law and the Internet" by L.A.Adamic and B.A.Huberman, Glottometrics, Vol. 3 (2002), pp. 143-150.   (Adamic & Huberman, 2002)

links to peers in order to get better – or more timely – information, therefore giving birth to clusters, dismantling the star.

On the other hand, scale-free networks are very robust. They have an inherent resistance to random failures. Barabasi and Bonabeau illustrate such robustness comparing what would happen with US highway system – a random network – versus what would happen to US airline system – a scale-free network – when the same number of nodes goes through an accidental (random) failure:

Random Network, Accidental Node Failure:

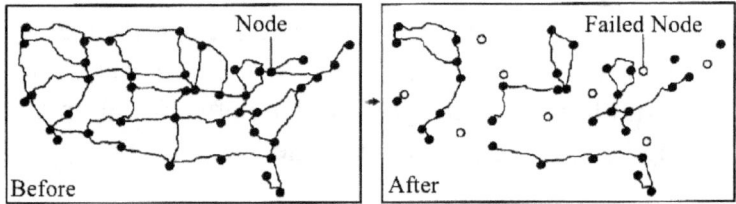

Scale-free Network, Accidental Node Failure:

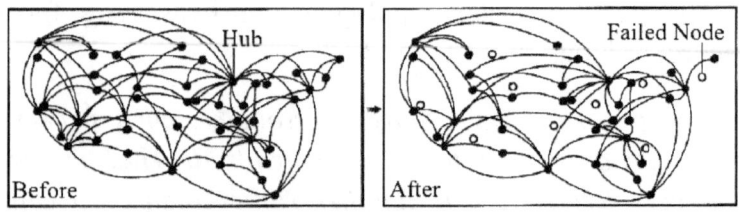

Figure 15: Accidental Node Failure. Radom and Scale-free Networks. (Barabasi & Bonabeau, Scale-Free Networks, 2003)

While random (Gaussian distribution) networks fall apart into non-communicating islands, scale-free network still keep its cohesiveness. *"As many as 80 percent of randomly selected Internet routers can fail and the remaining ones will still form a compact cluster in which there will still be a path between any two nodes."* [137]

Such robustness constitutes a significant advantage from an evolutionary perspective that can help us to explain the presence of scale-free networks and power law distributions in many different fields from biology to epidemiology, from sociology to economics.[138]

We are learning scale-free networks and power law distributions are more common than we once thought – probably because we were locked within our mass-average "normal" paradigm.

> Several theories explain power laws. Frequently they hinge on interdependence among data points and a possible ensuing positive feedback process. Herein lies the problem for 'normal' science: Most quantitative research involves the use of statistical methods presuming independence among data points and Gaussian 'normal' distributions... The trouble is that the many findings of power law phenomena across many natural and social sciences indicate that interdependent phenomena are far more prevalent than 'normal' statistics assumes and the consequent extremes have far greater consequence than the 'averages' in between.
>
> See "Beyond Gaussian Averages: Redirecting Management Research Toward Extreme Events and Power Laws"
> (Andriani & McKelvey, 2006)

---

[137] See "Scale-Free Networks" (Barabasi & Bonabeau, Scale-Free Networks, 2003)

[138] See "Using 'power curves' to assess industry dynamics" by M.Zanini, Nov'08. at mckinseyquarterly.com (Zanini, 2008)

Power laws are not new, but have been kept at bay for a considerable length of time. By the end of nineteenth century Pareto had already noticed that in a variety of different societies, regardless of countries or ages, the distribution of income and wealth followed a power law, which became popular as the 80/20 rule – 80% of wealth hold by roughly 20% of the population. In 1941 J.M.Juran popularized what he called "the Pareto principle" incorporating the 80/20 rule to his quality control theories stating that 80% of the defects come from 20% of the root causes – "the vital few and trivial many." [139]

Network theory has also been around for a while. Mathematician Leonard Euler wrote in the eighteenth century what is considered the first paper in graph theory when solving the so-called Königsberg bridges problem.[140] Sociology has been studying social networks since the beginning of the twentieth century. By the middle of the twentieth century, researchers connected mathematical graph theories to sociological studies of networks.[141] In 1959, Paul Erdos and Alfred Renyi developed a network model by connecting their nodes with randomly placed links – bell-shaped distribution curves. And after that, *for more than 40 years, science treated all complex networks as being completely random.*[142]

---

[139] See "Using the (Juran) Pareto" by T.Arnold, Jan'03 at newsandtech.com (Arnold, 2003)

[140] Seven bridges connected the four different land masses in Königsberg, and the question was, "Is it possible to draw any single path that crosses all seven bridges exactly once each?" See more about it at Carl Spitznagel (Spitznagel, 2000)

[141] See Mathematical Sociology entry in Wikipedia.

[142] See "Scale-Free Networks" (Barabasi & Bonabeau, Scale-Free Networks, 2003)

"Why did the field of network research wait another 50 years to take off? The main problem the sociologists faced was the difficulty to create large reliable networks. ...they could not answer [their questions] in an adequate manner because of the poor experimental data." [143]

In 1998, Albert-László Barabási and colleagues at the University of Notre Dame, having this time computer power at their hands and a huge database – the Internet – to search, found out networks were not random but scale-free having connections distributed by a power law instead of a "normal" bell-shaped curve.

> Such discoveries have dramatically changed what we thought we knew about the complex interconnected world around us. Unexplained by previous network theories, hubs offer convincing proof that various complex systems have a strict architecture, ruled by fundamental laws that appear to apply equally to cells, computers, languages and society. Furthermore, these organizing principles have significant implications for developing better drugs, defending the Internet from hackers, and halting the spread of deadly epidemics, among other applications.
>
> See "Scale-Free Networks"
> (Barabasi & Bonabeau, Scale-Free Networks, 2003

That work, and the need to understand the Internet phenomenon, triggered an explosion of research on networks and power-laws:[144] improving the model, trying to better understand the growth dynamics of the networks,

---

[143] See "Complex Networks and Dynamics of an Information Network Model," (Rosvall, 2003).

[144] See "Taming Complexity" by A.Barabsi, Nature Physics 1, 68 - 70 (2005)

their fractal nature, their modularity, their clustering and their communities. As we work on understanding the inherent self-organization mechanisms in the networks, which lead them to become scale-free, we are finding out that these mechanisms possibly try to optimize the balance among the efficiency, the cost to handle information and the network robustness.[145]

Nevertheless, most questions are still open. No one can tell for sure how the World Wide Web will look like in the future. But we know that right now it looks like a scale-free network and its nodes follow a power law distribution and we also know that there is a good chance it will remain like that.

> **In a scale-free world we must be very aware of the outliers as they have more meaning than anything at the mean.**

In a scale-free world there is no meaningful average and we can't ignore the extremes beyond a few sigma deviation.

This represents a huge paradigm shift from the "normal" distribution Gaussian world. Rather than focus on the average and ignore the extremes, in a scale-free world we must be very aware of the outliers as they have more meaning than anything at the "mean." [146] Rather than a snapshot of a stable "Gaussian" curve we need a dynamic view of the landscape – how it is growing, how links are establishing, how clusters or communities are forming.

---

[145] See "Complex Networks and Dynamics of an Information Network Model," (Rosvall, 2003).

[146] Our language, one more time, denoting our Gaussian way of thinking...

But if we are moving from a Gaussian world to a scale-free world, what do we do with our old molds and their required averages?

The simple answer is: We can break most of them.

The mold idea is a breakthrough that transformed our civilization. By allowing us to replicate an original book into thousands of copies it increased exponentially the book reach and permanence. Once we got a larger, more accessible and cumulative base of knowledge we accelerated the innovation process and increased exponentially societies' productivity and output.

But the mold idea and its breakthrough formula – one design, one mold aiming to an average consumer, mass production, mass advertising, and mass distribution – can now be replaced by a better idea.

We don't need any more to print a book so thousands of people can read our thoughts. We don't need to wait a long cycle until somebody that has a relevant contribution to that thought has a chance to publish it in another book or article or paper.

> Now we can have the reach and the permanence of the mass mold but with the speed and fluidity of the old conversations.

Now we can have the reach and the permanence of the mass mold but with the speed and fluidity of the old conversations. And even better: as this conversation now can be held by so many people at once, the quality of the arguments and the knowledge involved is multiplied manifold.

In the literate-mass-media era, problems had a long way to go until they could find their solutions. They eventually would find them, as knowledge was steadily accumulated. But a scientist or a researcher within a company had limited chances to debate with the right people who could lead to the solution they needed. The knowledge required – or the spark of creativity – could be somewhere else in the world and it could take a long time – or a few generations – until they could find each other.

> " In the literate-mass-media era, problems had a long way to go until they could find their solutions. The knowledge required – or the spark of creativity – could be somewhere else in the world and it could take a few generations until they could find each other.

Maybe we will still need molds and averages in the manufacturing of physical goods, despite the fact that we have been moving towards segmentation and micro-segmentation. But we won't need them when dealing with information goods or services. We can break the mold of advertising[147] and we can break the old mold of distribution.[148] In the scale-free world instead of pushing products onto the physical shelves trying to meet the average consumer's demand we will have a pull system with digital shelves customized for each customer.

This is already starting to happen. Think of Google, for example. We type what we are looking for. It provides us a rich customized shelf, offering many possible answers with different approaches and different perspectives, from

---

[147] See chapter six: The Crumbling Advertising Mold
[148] See the chapter ten: The Digital Shelf

scholarly papers to popular suggestions. Some time ago, when we wanted a song, we had to buy also all the other songs coming in the same CD. Now we just go to iTunes. Our shopping cart carries exactly what we want; even a customized song with our name in it, if we want it.[149]

We are at the end of the era of molds and averages. For a few centuries they multiplied our productivity and our overall output, releasing us time to think.

Now we are going through another breakthrough. The digital medium allows us to keep the permanence and reach brought by the printing press while bringing back the fluidity and speed of the old village conversations. The digital medium multiplies manifold the ease with which information can be spread.

James Burke's words:

> *..the ease with which information can be spread is critical to the rate at which change occurs.*[150]

Accelerated innovation drives major improvements in production processes, products and services, delivering much more for much less.

---

[149] See "Jessica Simpson sings for you with new customized songs," by Humphrey Cheung (Cheung, 2006) or a CD of songs customized with your child's name at www.nameyourtune.com

[150] See the book "Connections," page 291 (Burke, Connections, 1978)

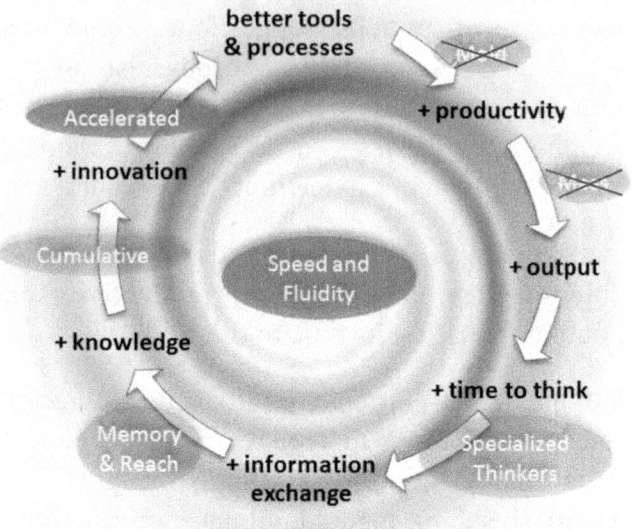

Figure 16: The digital medium is accelerating
the innovation/productivity virtuous cycle

In this scale-free world creativity is in the mesh. Debate is
part of Internet's nature. It has the structure that can put
market mechanisms to match problems demand with supply
of solutions – not one size fits all, but a specific solution
addressing anyone or any company need. And these market
mechanisms can get more effective over time, helping
people to find who wants their product, their service, their
creativity, their labor.

A more effective labor market[151] – matching labor demand
with supply – can make it easier for people to spend their
working time doing what they do better and what they like

---

[151] Take a look at "Mom-and-Pop Multinationals" by Pete Engardio,
Jul'08 at Business Week web site. (Engardio, 2008) See also "Future
Labor Markets - Technology Assessment" by H.Varian,J.Hall, M.Jain,
S.Lee, A.Pechon, K.Skucha, M.Wise, (Varian, et al., 2007)

most – getting a fair market price for that. Engagement levels can soar, further fueling overall society productivity.

We are at the edge of another large leap in our civilization efficiency. We are at the edge of an era when people can have a better chance to work on what they do better and what they like, and when machines and processes can do a lot more for a lot less.

It seems we are at the edge of an era that is poised to become the era of abundance. Will we be able to leverage it? Will we be able to make it happen? Or are these changes bringing other implications that will make our lives worse rather than better?

Throughout history we have learned no revolution is entirely for good or for bad and each person will have a different understanding depending on each one's perspective.

The ones looking for an egalitarian world where everyone gets a close-to-the-average share of wealth or a close-to-the-average share of attention – or importance – will probably be disappointed. On the other hand, those who are tired of the averages and of its disregard for what or who is out-of-the-norm will probably feel liberation.

Despite its democratizing effect breaking the hegemony of the top-down mainstream media, reinforcing the weight of people's opinion, opening a two-way channel for ever-evolving debates, the Internet will not flatten the business world, nor feed egalitarian ideals. Rather than bringing people close to the average, the Internet is more about taking care of the outliers.

Rather than egalitarianism, democracies are more about opening up and expanding the role of public opinion, giving people a chance to vote, to talk and to participate. They are not about building egalitarian societies. They are more about the process dynamics rather than the snapshot of the final estate. The original architects of modern democracies probably didn't have in their minds many of the today's achievements that we take for granted.

> The history of the US illustrates the way in which a society that concerned itself largely with the happiness of property-owning white males could gradually and peacefully change itself into one in which impoverished black females have become senators, cabinet officers, and judges of the higher courts. Jefferson and Kant would have been bewildered at the changes that have taken place in the Western democracies in the last two hundred years. For they did not think of equal treatment for blacks and whites, or of female suffrage, as deducible from the philosophical principles they enunciated.
>
> See "Democracy and Philosophy" at Eurozine.com
> (Rorty, 2007)

The democratic nature of the Internet has led many people to believe the Internet would flatten the landscape leading to an increase of the importance of small businesses, causing the fall of the old businesses empires and redistributing more uniformly the wealth across the industries.

Of course old business empires can – and will – disintegrate if they don't get rid of old paradigms and learn how to deliver what people are demanding in this new era. But the chances are that new multibillion dollar – or even bigger multitrillion dollar[152] – companies will replace them. This is what we should expect in a power law distribution.

In a power law distribution, in a scale-free world, there is no egalitarian distribution of wealth. The rich get richer. On the other hand, there is no a "winner-that-takes-it-all." There is no discontinuity. *"The largest step function in a power law is between #1 and #2 positions, by definition. There is no A-list that is qualitatively different from their nearest neighbors, so any line separating more and less trafficked* [sites] *is arbitrary."* [153]

So should we surrender to the power law and renounce our fair world ideals?

Only if we believe fairness means equality. Otherwise we have good reasons to believe the Internet scale-free network can help on improving the world fairness. There was more opportunity in the mass media world to fabricate unfair success than there is now in the World Wide Web. Popularity is getting harder and harder to fake and very easy to lose. In the new system, popularity is a result of distributed approval across the web rather than a constrained and elitist editorial selection.[154]

> 66 People have greater chance now to bubble up. The viscosity of the system has dropped to a large extent.

Of course there are still people deserving more than what they are getting. But they have greater chance now than they

---

[152] See "The cloud's best-kept secret" by Hugh McLeod, Aug'08 at gapingvoid.com (Macleod, 2008)

[153] See "Power Laws, Weblogs, and Inequality," Feb'03, in Clay Shirky's blog. (Shirky, 2003)

[154] For more on this topic see reference above.

had before, to bubble up. The viscosity of the whole system has dropped to a large extent.

If we look at the power law distribution through a static snapshot we will become prey to the old Gaussian world paradigm and incur in at least two mistakes.

First mistake, we would be tempted to conclude that as 20% of the items – sites, people, etc., – account for 80% of the results, we should focus on these 20% and pay little or no attention to the rest. This is what Juran suggested in the 1940s through the Pareto Principle: *"the vital few and the trivial many."*

Second mistake, we would focus our discussion on the shape of the curve. We would discuss fairness in terms of the shape of the distribution considering a fat head (or tail depending on how you plot the axes) – with a higher share for the "other 80%" – would be less unfair.

But snapshots are misleading and understanding scale-free networks requires a dynamic view of the landscape. *"What matters is not the size of the ruling elite, it's how they got there."* [155]

So it is not the curve shape that matters but the dynamics of the network and the fluidity and speed of the system.

On the first mistake, if we focus on the top 20% and give little attention to the other 80% we will be staring at a snapshot of aging successes and we will miss all the action

---

[155] See "The Real Long Tail," by Anand Rajaraman Jul'08 at his blog: Datawocky. (Rajaraman, 2008)

that is going on through the rest of the network, which is conceiving the future generation of successes.

On the second mistake, if we focus on the portrait of the curve shape we will think of fairness related to how many people are at the top. But if we focus on the network dynamics we will think of fairness related to how fast the people – who deserve it – move to the top, and how fast people – who don't deserve it anymore – get back to the bottom.

So, should we leave it to the power laws to determine how much each one should get?

We never did. Our society is not a result of the power laws. It is the other way around. Power laws are a result of the way we interact, our interdependencies and feedbacks.[156]

For the whole of human history we have been struggling to find out the best balance between market freedom and institutional interventions. We have learned through time such balance lies somewhere in the middle.

Too much freedom can lead to escalating quarrels, which break the market apart.[157] So we need institutional interventions to reduce the friction, to lubricate the market fostering a common ground and as consequence fostering efficiency and productivity. In the other hand too many rules kill creativity and stiff evolution.

---

[156] Take a look at "The Tyranny of Power Law and Why we Should Become Eclectic" at Econophysics blog Jul'06. (Econophysics, 2006)
[157] Take a look at this interesting paper that talks about the dynamics that lead Amazon tribes to split after they reach a critical size, by R.L.Carneiro, Sep'00 at pnas.org (Carneiro, 2000)

We will need to learn on-the-go how much we want regulate the Internet, in order to take the most of it, the same way we have been learning how big we want our governments to be, keeping in mind that a *"government has nothing to give anybody except what it first takes from somebody, and a government that's big enough to give you everything you want is big enough to take away everything you've got."* [158]

We will need to review our institutions (not just businesses, but also educational and governmental) because they are largely designed for a Gaussian world.[159] *"We need to free ourselves from 'average' thinking."*[160] *"...observing outliers may be more informative than observing average or typical entities."* [161] Or as we stated before: In a scale-free world, outliers have more meaning than the mean.

We will need to learn how to better deal with the scale-free networks and power law distributions so we use them for the best of society.

This new era has the potential to deliver a steep increase on our civilization productivity and wealth. Information can now spread easier than ever and the rate of change can intensify resulting in accelerated innovation and improvements in our production processes.

---

[158] See "Seven Principles of Sound Public Policy" by L.W.Reed at Mackinac.org (Reed, 2006)

[159] See "The power of Power Laws" by John Hagel, , May'07, at his blog: Edge Perspectives with John Hegel. (Hagel, 2007)

[160] Anderson, P.W. (1997) 'Some Thoughts About Distribution in Economics', cited at (Andriani & McKelvey, 2006)

[161] Meyer, A.D., Gaba, V. and Colwell, K.A. (2005) 'Organizing Far from Equilibrium: Non-Linear Change in Organizational Fields' cited at (Andriani & McKelvey, 2006)

The way we redefine our current institutions will play a vital role on our ability to harvest such potential. It will affect the balance between the predictions made by the pessimists and the optimists.

No revolution is entirely for good or for bad, but all instigate some pessimism or optimism depending on each one's perspective. And both, the pessimists and the optimists, play a very important role as we build our future.

The optimists call attention to the potential we have ahead of us and feed creativity. The pessimists call attention to the risks and feed institutional reforms.

So is this new era coming for good or for bad?

The optimists are talking about widespread information and speed of innovation. *"It took us fifteen years to sequence HIV, we sequenced SARS in 31 days,"* says Ray Kurzweil.[162] They are talking about how we are moving to a more fair society, with less room for kleptocracies.[163] How we are moving into a new civic sphere where widespread knowledge across society will bring better political balance. How people are becoming less passive, more combative and participative on issues that matter to them (read more about that on the last chapter of this book).

The pessimists are talking about digital and social divide, about a world where an elite has access to all innovations – like cognitive and genetic enhancements, extended life

---

[162] See "Heaven or Hell? How will technology shape our future?" (CNN, 2006)

[163] Government characterized by corruption; ruled by thief or thieves.

span, and so on – while a population of have-nots grow resentment increasing the risks of social upheavals.

The optimists are talking about a new era when people are back to the villages where they are not averages but individuals, where conversations are replacing the mass media one-way-flow despotism, where they can express themselves.

The pessimists are talking about walled gardens. About an era when people get back to their villages and close themselves inside, surrounded by *"comforting and confirming information and utterly shut out anything that conflicts with* [their] *world view,"* incurring the risk of *"huddling into tribes defined by shared prejudices."* [164]

The optimists are talking about a world where people know each other by a name not by an ID number. The pessimists are talking about a world where no one has any privacy.

The optimists are talking about a world where people will have any information at reach and an incredible ability to sift through it, discarding clutter and enhancing their cognitive and creative skills through a multilayered collaborative process.

The pessimists are talking about a world where people are self-centered and shallow,[165] have very short attention spans and are superficial not just in their perception of the world but also in their relationships.[166]

---

[164] Paul Saffo cited at (Economist, <u>What sort of revolution</u>?, 2006)
[165] Take a look at the "<u>Epic 2015</u>" video (Sloan & Thompson, 2005)
[166] Take a look at "<u>Is Google Making Us Stupid</u>?" by N.Carr, Jul'08 at theatlantic.com (Carr N. , 2008)

The pessimists are asking: If music companies go bankrupt who will take care of producing the good quality songs today sold in iTunes? If Newspapers go bankrupt who will produce the good-quality and reliable reports you can find today through Google or any other news aggregator?

The optimists are saying: At the beginning of this digital era, we are already seeing more people producing music and news than we have ever had. Of course prices can go down if supply is higher than demand but this is how society gets better, not worse. More productivity leads to lower prices and abundance. A sector or a region or a country can get worse if it relies too much on the lowered-price product or service but in a global scale more will be produced for less.

The pessimists are saying: Maybe the sheer volume can go up – fed by millions of user-generated-content – but the quality will go down, as they will be generated by amateurs if professional media outlets go bankrupt.

The optimists are saying: If there is demand, there will be supply. If people demand quality, quality will be there.[167] But it will be a quality defined by the people, not by autocratic editorial filters. After all, if quality definition had to follow top-down editorial filter, jazz and rock 'n roll

---

[167]In Rupert Murdoch (chairman of News Corp.) words: "Media companies don't control the conversation anymore… Quality is more important than ever, because the marketplace is more ruthlessly competitive… Old media can survive – and thrive – in this new environment, but they must adapt. We most learn how younger generations of consumers prefer to receive their news and entertainment, and we must meet those expectations…"
See "Mixed Media" by Rupert Murdoch, May'07 at Forbes.com (Murdoch, 2007)

would still be waiting in line for their chance at the classical music stage.

So, who is right? The pessimists or the optimists?

In the Gaussian world you can aim at a target, plot a 'normal' distribution and calculate your margin of error. Your shots are independent variables and the target is there, just waiting for you to guess it correctly.

> " In the networked world of power laws, the variables are interdependent and the future is a moving target that is affected by each guess we make.

In the networked world of power laws, the variables are interdependent and the future is a moving target that is affected by each guess we make. Rather than try to measure accuracy – who is right or wrong, the pessimists or optimists – against a deceptive non-static target, we do better understanding the dynamics of the system and how our guesses can affect it.

In such a world, as pessimists and optimists debate, ideas get connected to actions, reshaping our institutions, and building a future that will be neither the pessimists' nor the optimists' scenarios. But it will have elements of both. And if the interdependencies and feedback loops in our big scale-free network were good enough to consider properly the risks pointed out by the pessimists, maybe we will be fortunate to have a future that is closer to the optimists' dream.

EIGHT

Mapping the Media Pipelines

This chapter presents a parallel between the buckets and pipes carrying water and the many mediums carrying content. Then it presents a map showing all different "media pipelines" that pump media products into our homes with the respective media repositories (storage) and media players (TV, stereo, VCR, DVD player, etc.).

In the past, music was something you heard and experienced – it was as much a social event as a purely musical one. Before recording technology existed, you could not separate music from its social context. Epic songs, and ballads, troubadours, courtly entertainments, church music, shamanic chants, pub sing-alongs, ceremonial music, military music, dance music – it was pretty much all tied to specific social functions. It was communal and often utilitarian. You couldn't take it home, copy it, sell it as a commodity... Music was an experience, intimately married to your life. You could pay to hear music, but after you did, it was over, gone – a memory

See "Survival Strategies for Emerging Artists and Megastars" by David Byrne at Wired, Dec'07 (Byrne, 2007)

The same is true for getting the news, hearing stories, discussing ideas. Those were social affairs. We had to go to the source, do it live. Those were events, not content. News, stories, ideas, music, couldn't be carried around; they simply happened. They relied on interactions among people and the sound of their voices and instruments - an evanescent sound, *which has meaning at the exact moment it was going out of existence.*[168]

It was like getting the water right at the stream: a social experience, which would be different every time, depending on the weather, on the season, on who was drinking or swimming with you.

One day we learned how to carry water inside buckets to use it in our house. Then we learned how to store it in our home water tanks. And after that we learned how to transport water within water pipes so we didn't need to carry the buckets any longer.

The same way, we learned how to store and carry ideas, stories and music. Before that, we had to go to the stream in order to experience them live. But then came the books, the vinyl, and the film. These are like buckets that we can use to store and carry ideas, stories, music, images and movies. And after that, we got radio waves and TV waves. These came like pipes bypassing the old buckets.

By the beginning of this twenty-first century, our homes are being flooded with ideas, stories and music that are pumped into them by different media pipelines. TV and Radio shows are pumped through the airwaves or cables. DVDs, CDs, Tapes, Games and books are pumped into our homes through the Retail pipeline. We go to the stores, we buy

---

[168] See "Writing Electronically : The Effects of Computers on Traditional Writing" by S.P.Ferris (Ferris, 2002)

them and we take them home as if we were carrying buckets of water – the medium is the bucket, the water is the content. Once they get inside, they can go to a storage place or we can enjoy them with the help of different electronic devices that can play each different medium.

Because different mediums require different pipelines, different media players and different storage, our houses are also flooded by diverse electronic devices.

If we map the media pipelines getting into our homes, the repositories where we store the different mediums, and the electronic devices we have to extract their content, our living room, or our home theater would look like that:

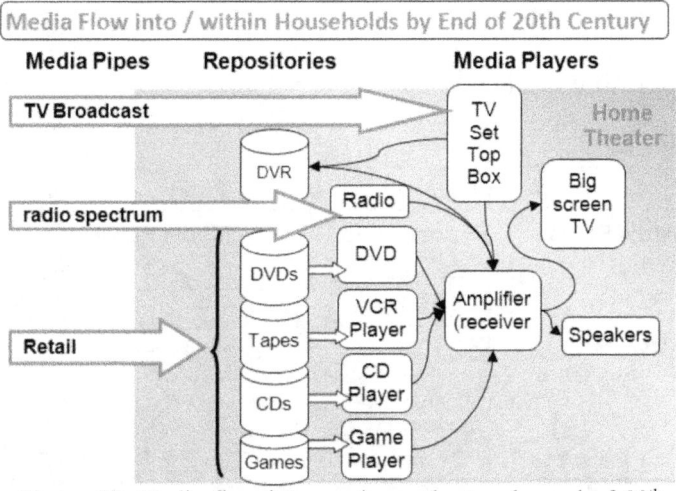

Figure 17: Media flow into our home theaters by end of 20th century

At this point we carry our content through the house as we used to carry water in buckets. If we want play in our home theater that DVD that we store in our bedroom shelf, we need to go upstairs and get it.

Our home office map:

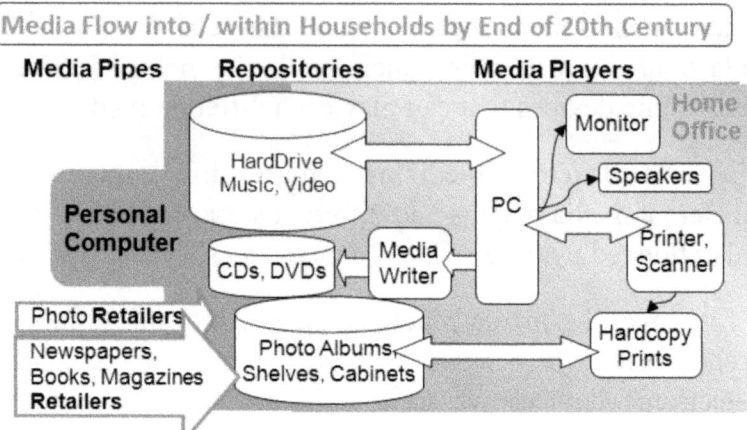

Figure 18: Media flow into our home offices by end of 20th century

Our portable devices:

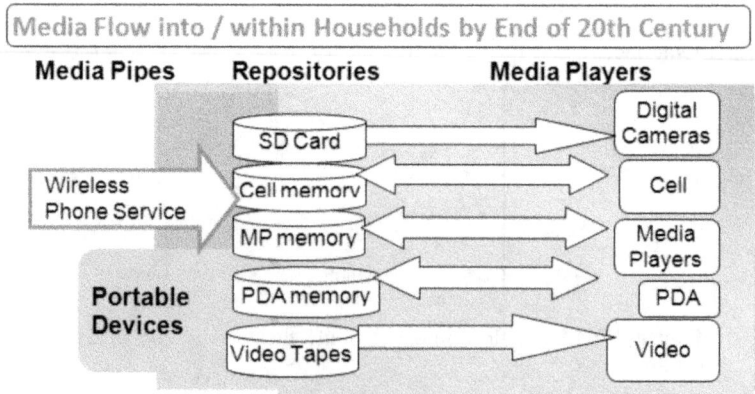

Figure 19: Media flow into our portable devices by end of 20th century

See the mapping of the whole house on the next page.

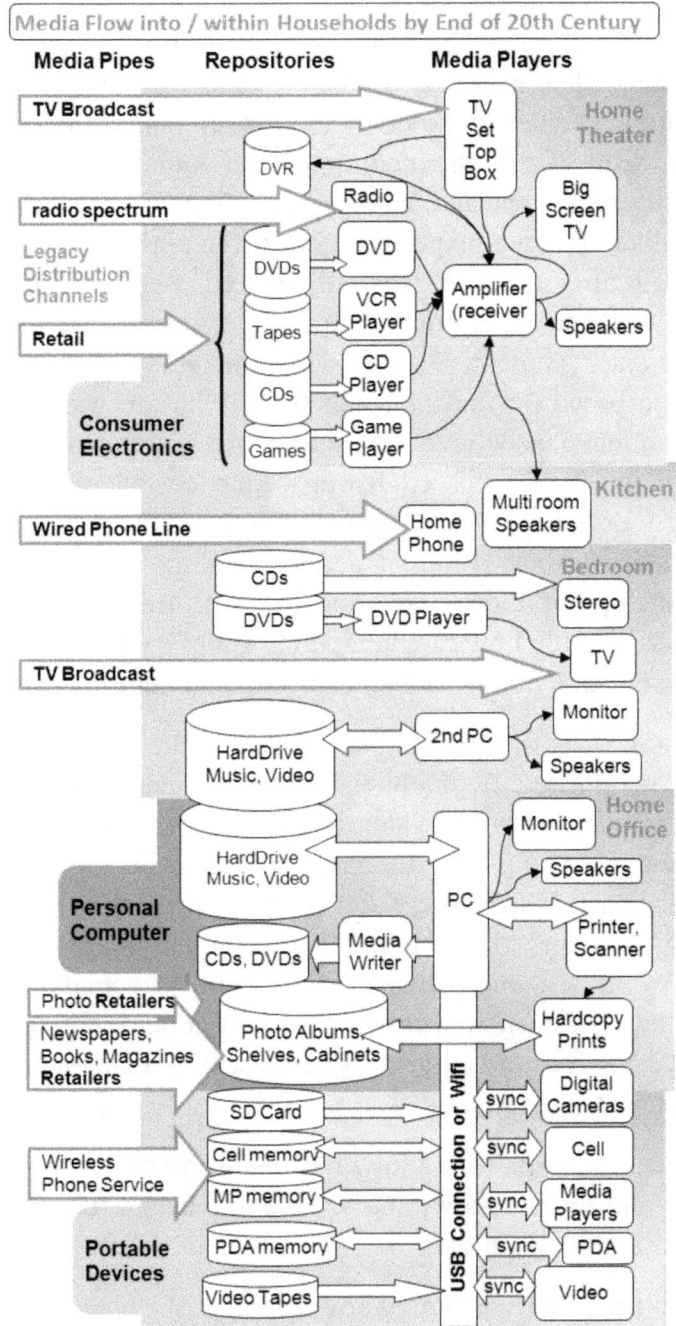

Figure 20: Media flow into our homes by end of 20th century

At this stage, the "content" word is very appropriate to describe what is being carried by the different kinds of medium. The actual experience is frozen and packed – it is contained – within the medium. Better sound systems, high definition movies and huge screens try to make content look like an actual experience but it remains just a shadow of the real experience. It is still frozen, contained; it is the same sequence every time we play it or every time we read it; it is just "content." It can't debate with us and it does not change based on the inputs of those who are watching. It tries to make us believe we are drinking at the actual stream but it is just a recorded frozen sequence that will repeat itself indefinitely no matter what we do. Video games went one step further; different actions leading us to different scenarios, but those scenarios are still frozen pre-coded scenarios with limited interaction. Unless we are playing with somebody else – which brings in another dimension.

But now, a new pipe has been added to the system: the IP (Internet Protocol) pipeline. This is a very peculiar pipe with no parallel in the water distribution system. It is a pipe that can carry any kind of content, be it text, sounds, images or videos. It is as if the water pipe could carry many more things, beyond the water. At first, this pipe was very narrow. It was more like a straw than an actual pipe. It couldn't allow enough flow to support good quality videos or even images or sounds. So, text was the main element in its circulatory system.

But, very fast, its technology has being improved providing more and more bandwidth. And people began to notice its power and implications.

In the next four chapters we will look at the characteristics and implications of this new medium.

NINE

The Hypermedium

In this chapter we talk about how the new digital pipeline, the Internet, is on the edge to replace all the other pipelines, becoming the dominant medium of a new era. We see how its multimedia capability and its two-way flow can simplify the information supply chain, connecting the scattered storage inside our homes, eliminating the need for most media players (TV, stereo, VCR, etc.) and eventually for the personal computer. We discuss how the retail role will change. When most information goods get delivered through the Internet, stores role can become more about featuring the full experience, encompassing the service plus the physical interface, rather than selling on the spot.

Record stores falling victim to Internet downloads, easy online access
September 7, 2008, Memphis Commercial Appeal
The handwritten sign informing customers that Cat's Music & DVD's in Midtown has closed its doors for good after 20 years tells an all-too-familiar story for slumping small-chain record shops…

"It's the same old story: declining sales," Wallace said. "There are so many ways to get your music now through the Internet…"

Sam no longer the record man in Halifax
February 20, 2007, CBC News
Sam the Record Man, a mainstay in downtown Halifax
for more than 20 years, is closing down Tuesday...

Co-owner Bobby Sniderman, son of founder Sam
Sniderman, said sales at the store on Barrington Street
are down, which he blames on music downloading.

In 2007 in US, music sales through the Internet already
represented 23% of the total sales. At this trend, somewhere
between 2010 and 2012 most of the music getting into our
houses will come through the IP pipeline.

169

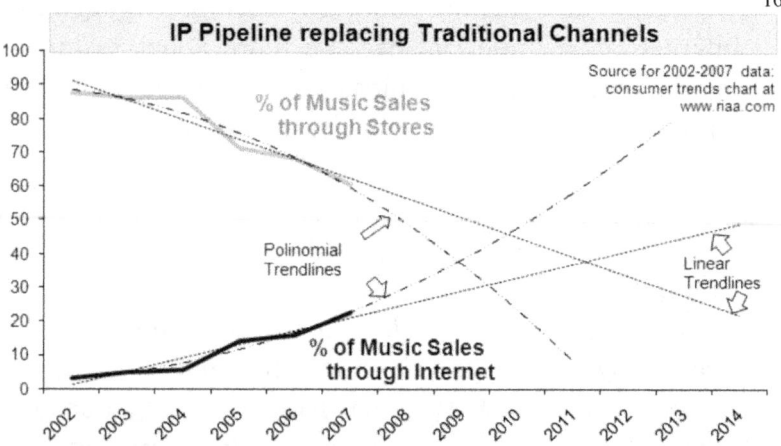

Figure 21: Music sales through Internet - projected crossover

As Internet connections with higher bandwidth are
deployed, more content is pumped into our houses through
the new IP pipeline replacing the traditional media pipes.
With declining volumes, stores that deal with information

---

[169] Chart built with data from Recording Industry Association of
   America (RIAA, 2007)

goods are forced to rethink their role in the supply chain or to close their doors.

"Philip Meyer, in his book 'The Vanishing Newspaper' (2004), predicts that the final copy of the final newspaper will appear on somebody's doorstep one day in 2043." [170]

The Internet is changing not just the channel through which the news is delivered but it is changing the very nature of the news. It *"has made the daily newspaper look slow and unresponsive."* [171]

> Rupert Murdoch, in a speech to the American Society of Newspaper Editors, in April, 2005—two years before his five-billion-dollar takeover of Dow Jones & Co. and the Wall Street Journal—warned the industry's top editors and publishers that the days when "news and information were tightly controlled by a few editors, who deigned to tell us what we could and should know," were over. No longer would people accept "a godlike figure from above" presenting the news as "gospel." Today's consumers "want news on demand, continuously updated. They want a point of view about not just what happened but why it happened... And finally, they want to be able to use the information in a larger community—to talk about, to debate, to question, and even to meet people who think about the world in similar or different ways."
>
> See "Out of Print: The death and life of the American newspaper." at newyorker.com (Alterman, 2008)

---

[170] See "Out of Print: The death and life of American newspaper" by Eric Alterman, The New Yorker, Mar '08 (Alterman, 2008)
[171] Ibid.

Microsoft predicts that Internet will overtake traditional Television as the most consumed form of media in Europe sometime between 2010 and 2011.[172]

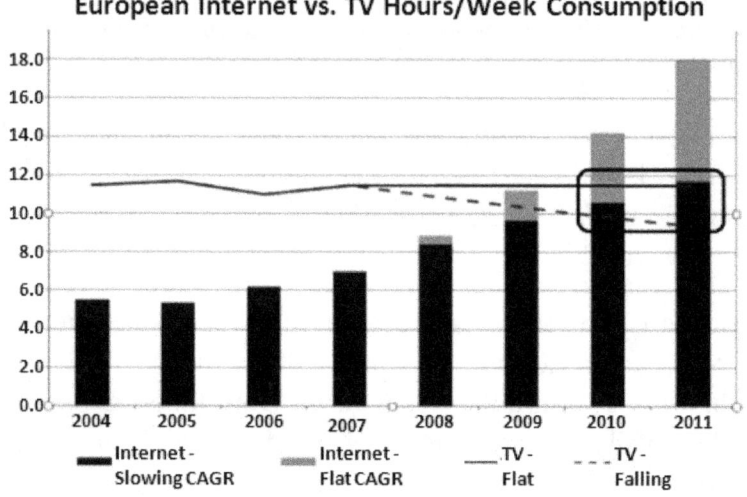

Figure 22: Media consumption - TV/Internet crossover (Microsoft, 2009)

Telephone landline is another medium that is suffering significant substitution by the IP Pipeline.

In January 2008, less than three years after launching an Internet voice service (VoIP – Voice over Internet Protocol), Comcast claimed it was already fourth largest phone service

---

[172] See "Will the Internet Overtake Television in 2010?" by Alain Thys, April 10, at FutureLab (Thys, 2009) or see the original source at "Europe Logs On – European Internet Trends of Today and Tomorrow," April 2009 by Microsoft (Microsoft, 2009)

provider in US, with 4.1 million subscribers.[173] By May 2008, Comcast already had 5.2 million subscribers.[174]

"In a study released today, [May 20, 2008] *TeleGeography reports that VoIP usage in the US reached 16.3 million subscribers in Q1 2008. That's 13.8 percent of all US households and 27 percent of all broadband customers."* [175]

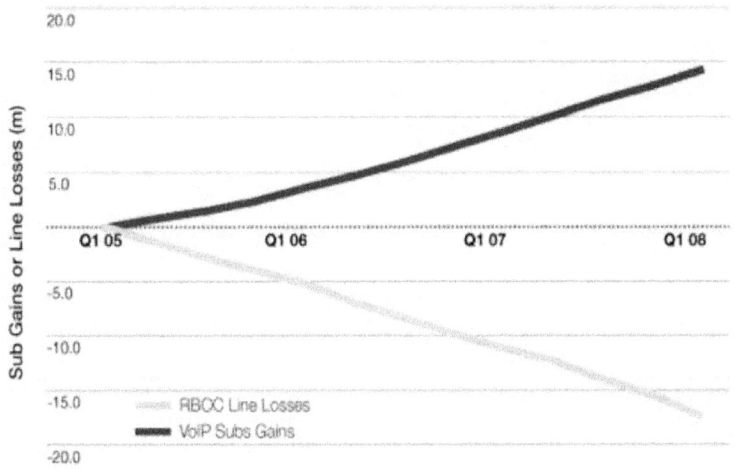

Figure 23: Traditional phone service drop vs. VoIP gain. (Chartier, 2008)

AT&T lost more than 2 million landlines from 2006 to 2007 and another 870 thousand in the first quarter of 2008. Verizon residential lines fell from 27.06 million to 24.11 million, a 10.9 percent decline since 2007. Qwest Lines fell

---

[173] See "Move Over Bells: Comcast Corporation Becomes the Fourth-Largest Phone Service Provicer In The US" from Comcast Press Releases. (Comcast, 2008)

[174] See "VoIP Ranking by Subscriber: Q1 2008" by Alex Goldman, Jul'08 at isp-planet.com (Goldman, 2009)

[175] See "VoIP joins cellular in eating away at telecom landlines" by David Chartier, Jul'08 at arstechnica.com. (Chartier, 2008)

from 8.63 million in March 2006 to 7.17 million in March 2008.

"At this rate of decline, within a few years the push-button wired telephone with service provided by a Bell company could be as rare and obsolete as a rotary phone is today."[176]

The IP pipeline will also replace TV broadcasting someday, once high bandwidth broadband is deployed.

Residential IPTV and VoIP Subscribers and Broadband Households in the US and Worldwide, 2007 & 2012 (millions)

	2007	2012
US		
IPTV	1.2	12.7
VoIP	17.5	33.8
Broadband	66.4	94.3
Worldwide		
IPTV	12.5	61.1
VoIP	69.6	196.3
Broadband	312.5	533.6

Note: IPTV includes all subscribers to an IPTV service whether they pay additional fees for it or not; VoIP includes paid subscribers only; broadband includes ADSL, cable, satellite, fixed wireless, fiber, powerline, WiMAX and emerging broadband technologies accessed at home
Source: eMarketer, April 2008

093430   www.eMarketer.com

Table 5: Broadband Services: VoIP and IPTV Trends (Macklin, 2008)

IPTV (Internet Protocol TV) already reached 12.5 million subscribers worldwide while Internet video services (like youtube) and movie rentals (like iTunes) are growing fast.

---

[176] See "Phones Without Homes: What's really killing the land-line telephone business" at slate.com (Gross, 2008)

Nevertheless it will take a while until the Internet can broadly replace TV broadcasting due to its huge bandwidth requirements, which can be above 20 Mbps (considering HDTV) as it was published in a study by the Broadband Stakeholder Group (UK) in May'06:[177]

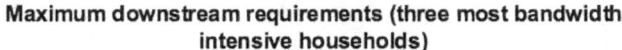

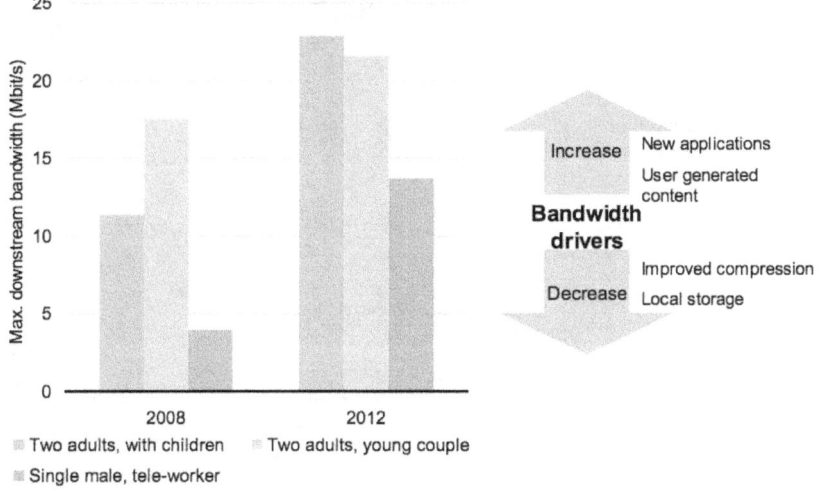

Figure 24: Projected Bandwidth Requirements by 2012 (BSG, 2006)

While the IP pipeline doesn't replace the traditional media pipes, the flow of content into and within our households will look like the figure in the next page.

Some content will also flow within the Home Network (through Ethernet cable or Wifi) and many coders and decoders will emerge to help throw content in one place in the IP pipeline and pick it up in another place.

---

[177] See "Predicting UK Future Residential Bandwidth Requirements" by BCG, May'06 at broadbanduk.org (BSG, 2006)

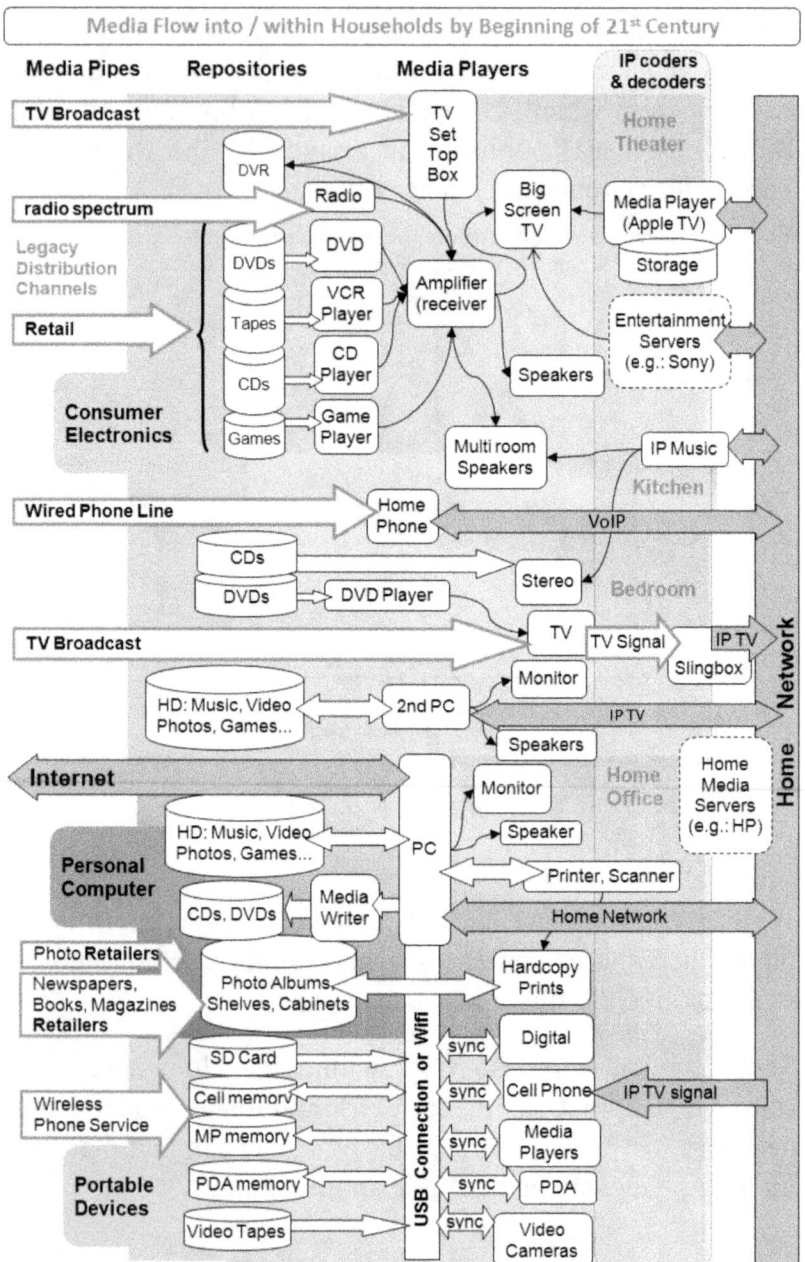

Figure 25: Media flow into our homes - IP coders and decoders

For a while, those coders and decoders will help us to couple our legacy consumer electronic equipment with the IP pipeline.

Like the Slingbox product that allows us to convert the TV broadcast – coming inside our house through traditional media pipes – into Internet Protocol packets, throw the signal into the IP pipeline and capture it back in any other place in the house or even out of the house in a piece of equipment (could be a laptop or a cell phone) connected to the home network or to the Internet.

Or like the Apple TV device that allow us to watch in our legacy TV, content coming from our computer or from the Internet. Or like the Apple Airport device that captures an mp3 music we've thrown in a wifi network and convert it into audio signals to be played in our legacy stereo in someplace else.

The day will come that those coders and decoders won't be needed anymore. At some point all our music will get into our homes through the IP pipeline. The same for radio, for telephone, for news and for TV.

Once the IP pipeline replaces the other media pipes, we also won't need the old traditional media players. Therefore most of the electronic devices we currently have to play our CDs, DVDs, Videotapes, TV programs, etc., are about to become obsolete. Once we get what we want from the web, we just need screens and speakers so we can see and hear.

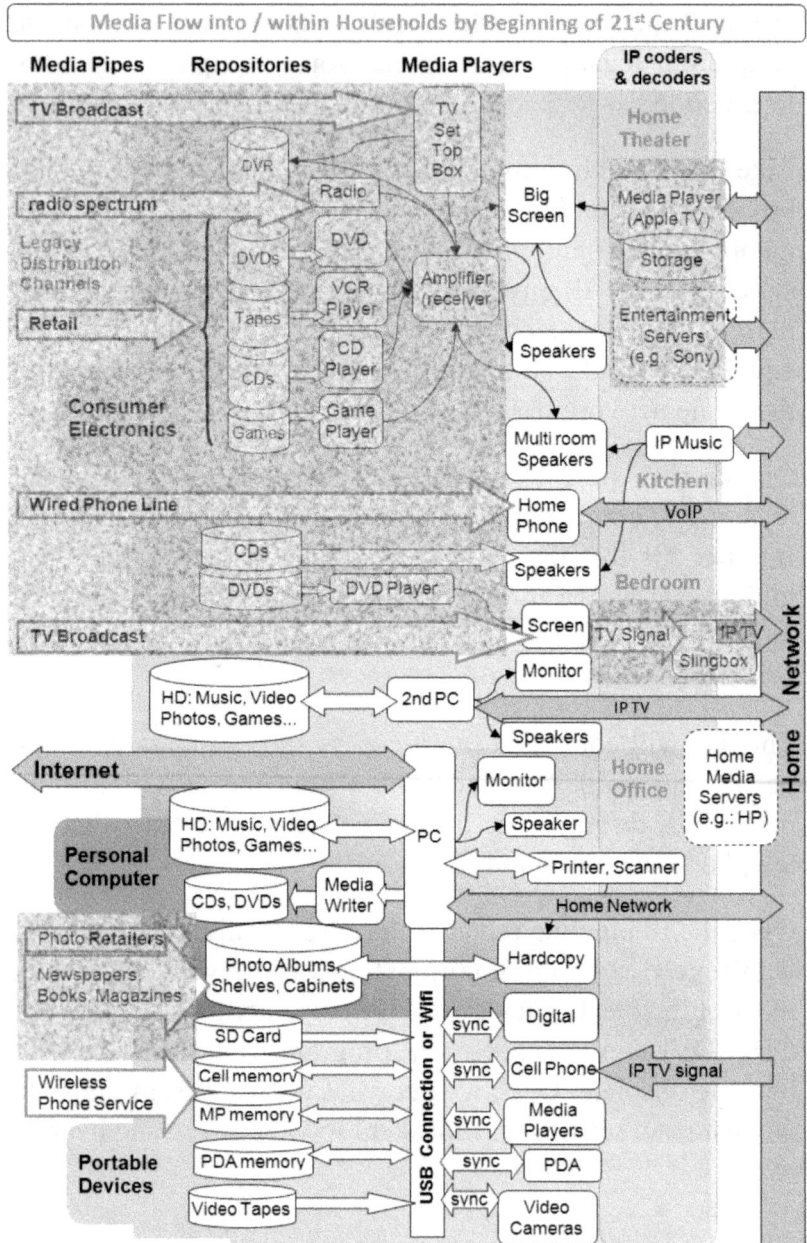

Figure 26: Media pipelines being replaced by the Internet

If the bandwidth is large enough, we don't even need much processing power on these displays, we can get everything already processed and adjusted to our screens, straight from the cloud.[178] All we will need will be devices with natural user interfaces acting like thin clients coupled to services in the cloud.

Will this scenario really happen? Probably not exactly like that and certainly not that fast. It requires high bandwidth and widespread broadband. It will take long for that to happen in some parts of the world. This scenario is just a vision to help us understand where the changes that are happening right now can take us. If we want learn with this scenario, probably the more instructive question is not "if" it will happen but "how long could it take" for the IP Pipeline to become the most important medium bringing information and entertainment within our lives? As we have seen, in some countries like the US it could be just a few years for music, another few years for news and a slightly longer for movies and TV programs.

In this vision, very little "content" will be sold through physical stores. Even the word "content" will become inappropriate because it relates to static packaged goods from the mass media era. The future will be more about events, conversation and services and less about pre-formatted information. (See chapter three – Back to the Village).

---

[178] See "How Cloud Computing is Changing the World," Aug'08 by Rachael King at businessweek.com (King, 2008) and "Google and the Wisdom of Clouds," Dec'07 by Stephen Baker at businessweek.com (Baker, 2007). See also the book "The Big Switch: Rewiring the World from Edison to Google" by Nicholas Carr (Carr, 2008a)

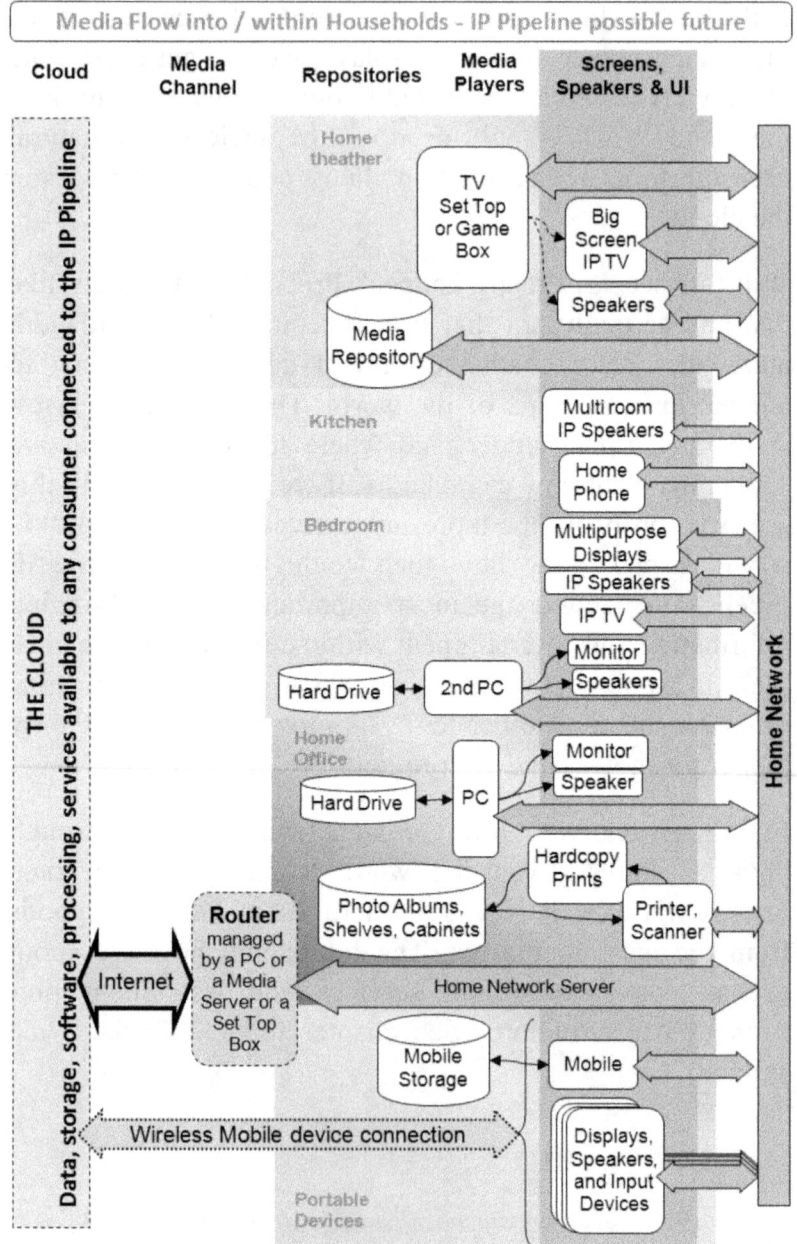

Figure 27: IP Pipeline – Possible future

Information goods can be showcased much better through the IP pipeline – consumers can find them, try them and buy them more efficiently than through a physical store.

But there will still be cases when the full experience can only be demonstrated through a specific physical device, like an iPod or an iPhone. Although the services and software can be downloaded through the Internet, we can only understand the full experience trying the iPod or the iPhone at the store. For Apple, it doesn't matter how many products the store is selling. What matter most is that it is providing people the opportunity to re-couple the "content" – or better, the service – with the medium so we can give it a try. Once we understand it, we can purchase it at the store or go back home and purchase it online. This brings a new dimension to the role of the physical store. It becomes a place to experience those products that mix Internet services with specific physical user interfaces, rather than a place for hard sales. It also helps us understand how critical and clever is the Apple distribution strategy.

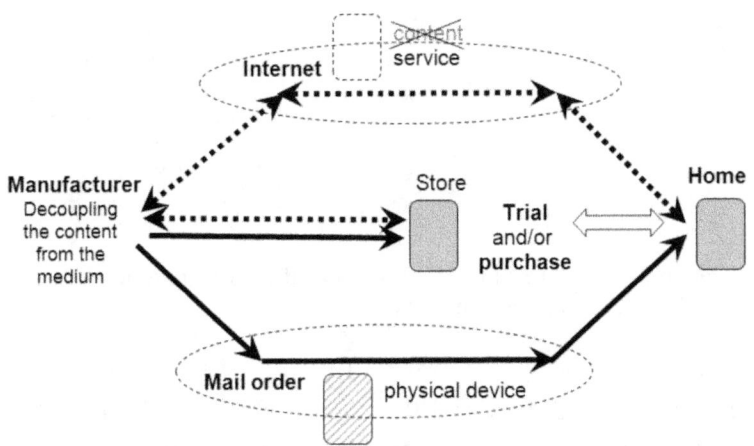

Figure 28: Decoupling the content from the medium – T h e Reshaping the Supply Chain

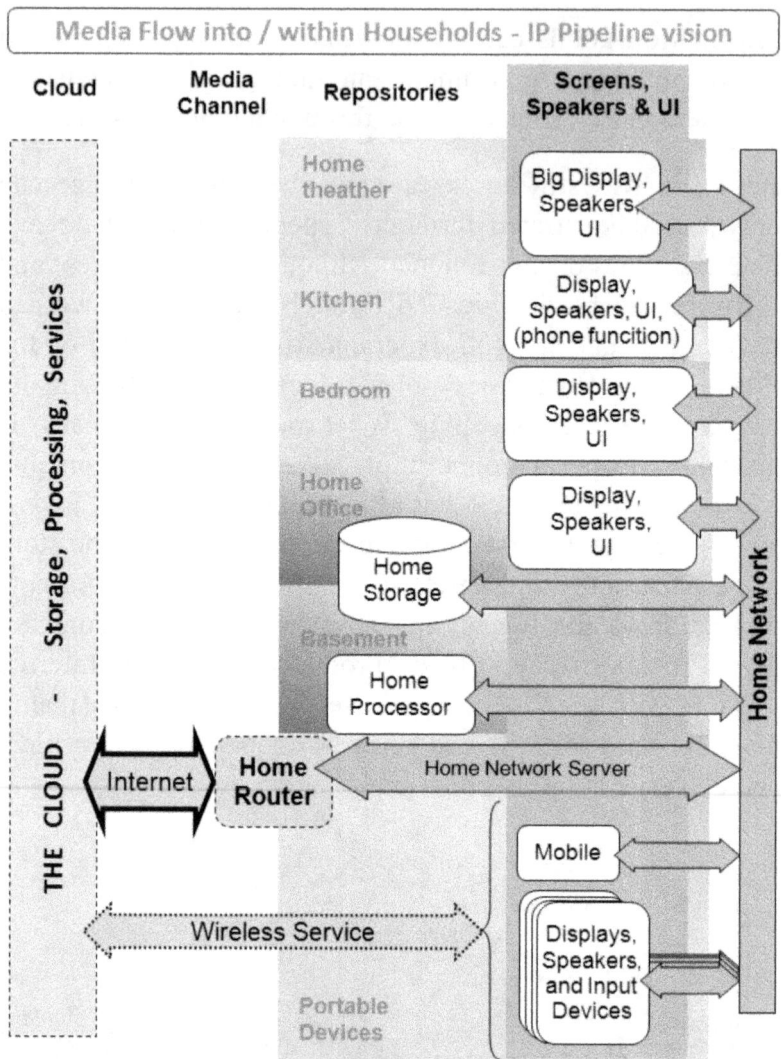

Figure 29: Future Simplified – Point of differentiation will be user interface and services delivered

figure above shows a simplified vision of the future, where the services, the data and the other people in the cloud are directly connected to our home network and to our wireless devices. All we need in this environment are screens, speakers and user input devices so we can see, hear, talk, type, gesticulate, while services are delivered to us, or we deliver services to others, or we just participate in our community conversation or in any other event.

As reliability grows we will have less need for local storage or even ownership. If we have a fast and reliable service at low cost, why should we own a song if we can have it played from the cloud anytime, anywhere paying just a penny for it? At this point, content – the song file – transmutes into an event almost AS in the old villages. If we can share the experience real time with other people online, it will be almost like watching, or listening to the live show.

> "As reliability grows we will have less need for local storage or even ownership.

The critical success factor for the companies in this vision will be defined by how good they are providing the services – not content – and coupling them with an outstanding user interface. The physical store role will be more about featuring the full experience than selling on the spot.

Even the Personal Computer, which has promoted many of these changes, will probably go away – at least in the way we know it. Maybe we will have a big home processor in the basement – more like an appliance – to which our screens around the house connect – like thin clients – so we can run programs or services no matter if the processing is happening at home or someplace else in the web.[179]

---

[179] See "Is PC era coming to an end? – New gadgets stealing their market," Nov'07, by Dave Parrack, at tech.blorge.com (Parrack, 2007) and "PCs losing their relevance in Japan," November 11th 2007, by By Hiroko Tabuchi, at usatoday.com (Tabuchi, 2007)

"Internet use on PCs will drop from 95% today to only 50% over the next 5 years as other web enabled devices such as IPTV, games consoles and mobile phones become more popular," says Microsoft.[180]

---

[180] See "Europe Logs On – European Internet Trends of Today and Tomorrow," April 2009 by Microsoft (Microsoft, 2009)

TEN

The Digital Shelf

In this chapter we talk about the autocracy of the physical shelf, how it plays in favor of the average mass products and against the niche products. We discuss how the new digital hypermedium, released from physical limitations, is democratizing the offering for physical goods. We take a look at the debate around the "long tail" concept, having in mind what we saw in chapter seven about scale-free networks. Then we see how, in the case of information goods, the digital medium goes one step further democratizing also the distribution and the means of production. As a consequence people are actively leveraging the two-way property of the digital medium, producing, distributing and accessing an increasing volume of user-generated-content suggesting the beginning of a new era of cultural richness and abundant choice.

The era of mass media is giving way to one of personal and participatory media. That will profoundly change both the media industry and society as a whole.[181]

Adam Bailey sings about the future. When he's not attending class at the University of Texas, the 18-year-old from Cedar Park is in the studio recording his original songs.

[181] Andreas Kluth in "Among the Audience," (Economist, 2006a)

The music bug bit him last year. He learned to play the piano and write songs. Like so many other musicians, his songs made their way on to the Internet for the entire world to hear and see.

His manager and recording producer, Scott Rehling, says it is now the fastest way to promote a musician and build a fan base: "With sites like MySpace, YouTube, and so forth, you create content of high quality, put it out there for the public, to the consumer directly via the Internet and sell it directly on the Internet."… "That's kind of the plan we have with Adam."…

It used to be that up-and-coming bands wanting to be discovered would send a tape or CD to record companies hoping theirs would make it to the top of the stack. Now with the Internet, bands cannot only be heard, they can be seen--and not just by a few…

See "Internet Allows Bands To Be Seen And Heard," September 12th 2007 (KEYETV, 2007)

The autocracy of the physical shelf

Before the water reaches consumers' faucets, it needs to fill the whole pipe, all the way from the city reservoir. If Adam wanted to have his music available for consumers before we had the Internet, he would need to fill the whole supply chain pipeline too. He would need to find a company wanting to produce CDs with his music, so they could sell them to distributors, which would sell those CDs to retailers, which would put them on their shelves waiting for consumers to pick them up and buy them. They would need to spend a good amount of money producing many CDs to fill this pipe if they wanted it available in a good number of stores' shelves.

They would need to spend more money on helping consumers know – through advertising – about the CD and where it was available.

They could lose all the money spent if they didn't succeed in making the right amount of product available at the right places or if they couldn't find the right people who would be willing to buy those CDs.

But even if they decided to take such risk, and to fill the pipeline, they would need permission to do it. Distributors and Retailers have very restrictive rules about including new products in their portfolios.

> Retailers' shelves follow strong hierarchies determined by mass market and economies of scale.

Retailers' shelves follow strong hierarchies determined by mass market and economies of scale. The products that sell more get more shelf space, more visibility and are present in more stores. The ones that sell less get less space, less visibility and fewer points of sale. This feeds a self-fulfilling prophecy boosting the sales of the top-sellers and making the small ones even smaller - until they lose the right to be on the shelf. Retailers are very selective on their assortment and shelf usage. In order to reduce the costs of their inventory – the water standing in the pipe – and to optimize their profitability, retailers don't want carry low volume selling products.

So most niche or new products don't have a chance to get a space in most of retailers' shelves. These niche products end up finding their way out through niche outlets and specialty stores. But they also have hard hurdles to overcome even within the specialty stores channel. The specialty stores also need some scale to pay their labor, inventory, and space, otherwise they would have to charge higher prices that could render their operation unviable.

In summary, retailers' shelves favor volume and mass-average, one-size-fits-all products and refuse low volume, niche products. Retailers' shelves require scale.

But the digital technology and the Internet are radically overturning this shelf autocracy by:
1. Democratizing the offering;
2. Democratizing the distribution and product trial;
3. Democratizing the means of production.

1. Physical Goods
– The democratization of the offering.

What if we could offer our products to consumers without the need to fill the whole pipeline?

We would have no costs of inventory, no costs of shelf space, no labor costs associated to physically handling the product.

What if we could decouple the consumer choice from product delivery? This way the physical movement of the product – and all costs associated with it – would happen only after the purchase was already secured. We would get rid of the high risk associated to niche and new products.

> "What if we could decouple consumer choice from product delivery?

This idea has been tried before, somehow, through catalog sales – a model successfully implemented by Aaron Montgomery Ward in 1872. As a traveling sales representative he realized he could build a successful business buying products direct from the manufacturers and selling them to farmers through mail-order catalogs. He launched his firm in Chicago with a $1,600 investment. By the time of his death his company's annual sales were $40 million.[182]

Mail order fueled the growth of some big companies (like Sears, Hammacher Schlemmer, Victoria's Secret and JC Penney) but its share of total retail sales remained relatively modest when viewed within the scope of the total retail trade and overall economic activity.

In 1988, the year that Dell Computer Corporation went public, the US mail order market represented 3% of total Retail sales. A small relative number but not negligible in absolute terms: a total of $164 billion dollars being $45 billion for business mail order sales, $42 billion for charitable and $77 billion for consumer mail order sales.[183]

Dell Computer Corporation sold 3.5 million shares at $8.50 a share, a total of almost 30 million dollars just four years after Michael Dell founded the company, with $1,000. In 1984, when he was a nineteen-year-old freshman at the University of Texas at Austin,[184] he had the idea he could do a good business selling computer components and kits by telephone and advertising in trade magazines. The idea

---

[182] See "Montgomery Ward" at Encarta.msn.com (Encarta, 2008)
[183] See "Mail order top 250+," Jul'89 at allbusiness.com Direct Marketing (DirectMarketing, 1989)
[184] Take a look at (E-Commerce Within Dell, 2004)

was based in the old mail order sales model. By eliminating the intermediary margins he would be able to compete with giants like IBM and Compaq that were selling through the traditional supply chain.

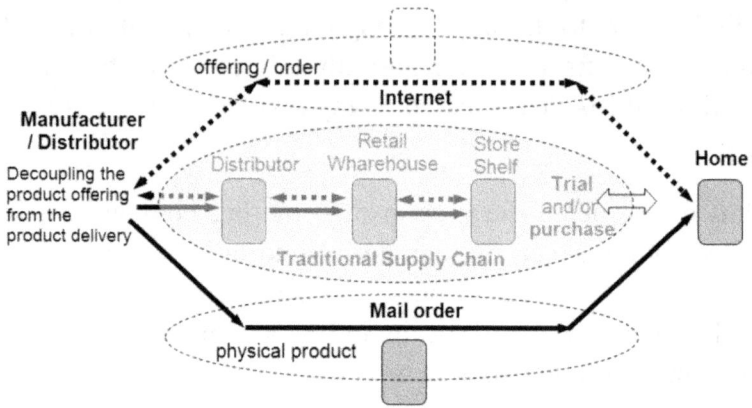

Figure 30: The Digital Shelf – Reshaping the Supply Chain
Physical Goods – Democratization of the offering

However, Dell went a few steps further enhancing the model. He not just delivered to order, but he also built to order, meaning that beyond not having to fill the whole supply chain pipeline, he didn't need to carry inventory himself.

While IBM and Compaq had to invest a good amount of money buying components, building computers, filling the supply chain, until they could get paid and until they could account for any return on that investment, Dell was getting the payment first. So he had the profit and the money needed to buy the components beforehand. No surprise he could grow so fast. He didn't even need to borrow money for working capital. His model has a negative working capital!

Other positive implications:

- High tech components lose value fast. Dell competitors could lose a great amount of money for higher priced components in their inventory.

- Dell could offer innovations faster while his competitors had first to get rid of old components and old products filling their long supply chain.

- Building to order, Dell could give customers a product closer to what they wanted.

- While IBM and Compaq contact with consumers was mainly indirect, Dell had direct everyday contact with all his consumers from whom he could learn and respond immediately, improving his products and services

- Direct contact with consumers allowed Dell not just to learn about their needs but also to shape their demand based on his needs (for example giving discount to 17" monitors if he had supply issues with 15" monitors).

When the Internet started to get momentum in the 90s, Dell had already set up a business model that could leverage the power of the new pipeline, using this new channel for direct sales and communication with his customers. He was one of the pioneers on offering his products through the Internet at his web site in 1994. But at that point consumers were still ordering by phone. He started online sales in 1996 and by 2000 he was selling $50 million a day online. In 2001 he surpassed Compaq, becoming the biggest PC seller in the world.[185]

---

[185] See "Dell changed the industry with direct sales" by John Pletz, at statesman.com. (Pletz, 2004) See also: "Internet sales boost Dell profits," Nov'98 at news.bbc.co.uk (BBC, 1998)

> More about Dell from "Living in the Dell Time" by Bill Breen at fastcompany.com (Breen, 2007):
>
> "Though it assembles nearly 80,000 computers every 24 hours, it carries no more than two hours of inventory in its factories and a maximum of just 72 hours across its entire operation."
>
> "Dell has achieved a cash-conversion cycle (that's the time between an outlay of cash for parts and the collection of payment for goods made from them) of negative 36 days. Hewlett-Packard doesn't disclose its cash-conversion cycle, but with its average of six weeks of inventory, the number is sure to be positive."
>
> "With just a few days' worth of parts on hand, Dell turns its inventory 107 times per year -- an astounding advantage over HP and IBM, which flip their inventories 8.5 and 17.5 times per year, respectively."

Internet became the key element in leveraging Dell's model. Despite mail-order catalogs' relative success, they are still severely restricted by the physical limitations of catalog size and catalog distribution. Catalog offerings are also considerably static, meaning, once published, it can take a considerable amount of time to change them.

Another company that fully understood the power of the Internet, since its earlier stages, as a democratic alternative to the despotism of retailer shelves was Amazon.com.

Amazon understood that the Internet allows anyone to put an offer to consumers without the need to spend upfront a huge amount of money filling the whole pipe and without the need to pass through distributors and retailers very restrictive filters dictated by the economies of scale. So, in 1995, Amazon launched its online bookstore.

By 2003, the number of book titles available at Amazon.com was already over 23 times larger than the number of books on the shelves of a typical Barnes & Noble **super**store and 57 times greater than the number of books stocked in a typical **large** independent bookstore.[186]

Suddenly any independent and unknown book author had a chance to display his or her book to millions who shop at Amazon. This phenomenon is well illustrated in the Wired magazine article, by Chris Anderson, which he called "The Long Tail:"[187]

> In 1988, a British mountain climber named Joe Simpson wrote a book called Touching the Void, a harrowing account of near death in the Peruvian Andes. It got good reviews but, only a modest success, it was soon forgotten.
>
> Then, a decade later, a strange thing happened. Jon Krakauer wrote Into Thin Air, another book about a mountain-climbing tragedy, which became a publishing sensation. Suddenly Touching the Void started to sell again.
>
> ...Now Touching the Void outsells Into Thin Air more than two to one...
>
> What happened? In short, Amazon.com recommendations.

---

[186] Data from the paper: "Consumer Surplus in the Digital Economy: Estimating the Value of Increased Product Variety at Online Booksellers," (Brynjolfsson, Hu, & Smith, 2006)

[187] See "The Long Tail" by Chris Anderson at Wired.com (Anderson, 2004)

The online bookseller's software noted patterns in buying behavior and suggested that readers who liked Into Thin Air would also like Touching the Void. People took the suggestion, agreed wholeheartedly, wrote rhapsodic reviews. More sales, more algorithm-fueled recommendations...

Particularly notable is that when Krakauer's book hit shelves, Simpson's was nearly out of print. A few years ago, readers of Krakauer would never even have learned about Simpson's book - and if they had, they wouldn't have been able to find it.

Amazon changed that. It created the Touching the Void phenomenon by combining infinite shelf space with real-time information about buying trends and public opinion. The result: rising demand for an obscure book.

Limited physical space and mass-market average thinking, dictated focus on the top sellers and little attention to the rest. Even a superstore with the size of a football field cannot fit much more than 100,000 titles while a typical large book stores carry between 40,000 to 100,000 titles. So it is natural they restrain their offering to what sells most.

The offering gets even more constrained when the superstores dominate the market causing the disappearance of the small independent stores,

At first sight, we could be led to believe that book superstores offering 100,000 titles are giving us more choices than independent stores offering only 20,000. But this math only works when we compare one store against another one. It does not hold true when we compare many superstores to many independent stores because the many superstores will probably have the same 100,000 titles defined by their headquarters (focusing on the bestsellers) while the independent stores will present much more diversity. The right math is more like this. One Barnes and Noble store: around 100,000 titles. Five hundred Barnes and Noble stores: around 100,000 titles. One independent bookstore: around 20,000 titles. Five hundred independent bookstores: some number from 20,000 – in the improbable case they all have the same titles – to 10 million – in the improbable case all the titles are different; most probably some number considerably below 10 million but considerably above 100,000.

Therefore at the time book superstores are replacing the smaller independent bookstores the bookshelf is becoming even more autocratic.[188]

The Internet came in a good moment to rescue the hundreds of thousands of titles falling out of the superstores cut.

But are those titles relevant?

Certainly not to mass-market superstores – for this reason they were left out. They sell less than the top 100,000. There isn't enough space in the physical shelves for them. Even though, some of them – like "Touching the Void" – can become a mass-market phenomenon if given a chance.

But they are relevant to Amazon and to the many buyers and sellers that now can find each other through the digital shelves. Around 25% of Amazon sales are composed of books ranked above 100,000, which for this reason wouldn't be able to get a space on the physical shelves of

---

[188] See "Read Between the Lines: Book superstores threaten the American literary future" by David Kornhaber (Kornhaber, 1999)

the book superstores.[189] If Amazon followed the superstores criteria, its sales would be 25% lower. And 25%[190] of Amazon buyers wouldn't be able to find what they wanted, and a huge amount of Amazon authors wouldn't be able to reach their readers.

By 2003, Amazon was already selling other categories beyond books extending the power of their digital shelves:

Product category	Amazon.com	Typical large brick-and-mortar stores
Books	2,300,000	40,000–100,000
CDs	250,000	5,000–15,000
DVDs	18,000	500–1,500
Digital cameras	213	36
Portable MP3 players	128	16
Flatbed scanners	171	13

Table 6: Virtual vs. physical store assortment
(Brynjolfsson, Hu, & Smith, 2006)

Chris Anderson's article was so successful that it led to a book, "The Long Tail, Why the Future of Business is Selling Less of More." The article and the book have generated a good amount of debate on whether the Internet will change the shape of the demand curve reducing the importance of the hits and increasing the relevance of the niches.

---

[189] (Brynjolfsson, Hu, & Smith, 2006) calculated 39.2% of sales of books ranked above 100,000 at Amazon but this figure has been reviewed. Chris Anderson's "The Long Tail" book claims it is around one quarter of the total.

[190] Rough simplification, assuming average prices for books above and below 100,000 are the same.

One indisputable point is: the digital shelf opens up space for the niche products. It opens up space for all those books beyond the 100,000 titles that do not fit within the book superstores' space and for all those songs that don't fit in the physical space available in a typical music store. In this sense the tail of the demand curve gets longer.[191]

The stronger dispute goes around whether the Internet changes the balance of power between the hits and the less privileged ones.

A simple answer would be yes, it does. Before the Internet if your book was ranked above 100,000 it would be out of the dominant book superstores shelves and therefore have a very tiny chance to be found by someone who would be willing to read it. So, the digital shelf gives a space and exposition that the less privileged ones didn't have before.

> "The digital shelf gives a space and exposition that the less privileged ones didn't have before.

But how significant is this power? Is it big enough to change the shape of the curve?

In one study, Prof. Erik Brynjolfsson, from MIT Sloan School of Management, and colleagues, compared traditional channels sales with internet sales and suggest that while the first follows the 80/20 Pareto principle, the Internet sales are less concentrated, having 80% of the lower ranked products generating 27.7% of the sales.[192]

---

[191] See "The Long Tail" (Anderson, The Long Tail, 2004)
[192] See (Brynjolfsson, Hu, & Simester, Goodbye Pareto, 2007)

The authors conclude: *"The balance of power will continue to shift from a few best-selling products to niche products that are previously difficult to be discovered by consumers. This Long Tail phenomenon will have a profound impact on a firm's product development strategy, operations strategy, and marketing strategy."*

Prof. Anita Elberse, from Harvard Business School, challenges such conclusion in the article: *"Should You Invest in the Long Tail? – It was a compelling idea: In the digitized world, there's more money to be made in niche offerings than in blockbusters. The data tell a different story."*

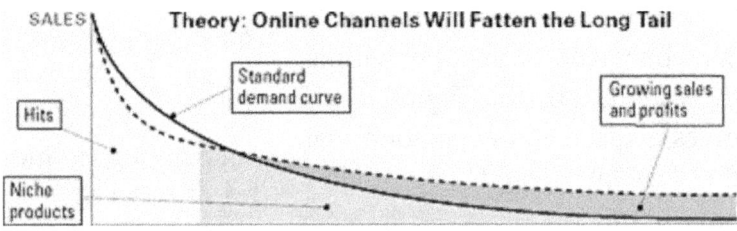

Figure 31: Reshaping the Long Tail? (Elberse, 2008)

Prof. Elberse argues the data she gathered on music and home video markets contradicts the long tail theory. In fact she sees more concentration happening than the other way around. *"...the tail is likely to be extremely flat and populated by titles that are mostly a diversion for consumers whose appetite for true blockbusters continues to grow."*

So, how is the long tail changing the shape of the demand curve? Does this question really matter?

We need to be careful when we consider what exactly are the questions we are trying to answer and from whose perspective. We need to be careful not to get locked into the old-normal-Gaussian paradigms. *"We need to free ourselves from 'average' thinking,"* and keep in mind that *"... observing outliers may be more informative than observing average or typical entities."* (see more about that on chapter seven: A Scale-free World, For Good or For Bad?)

So, is the Internet changing the balance of power between obscure items and the hits? Yes. Obscure items that had no-power-at-all now have a digital shelf that helps buyers meet the sellers. It is a less autocratic shelf. Now, instead of editorial filters, it is people's demand that defines the titles to be promoted to a higher rank.

> "We should be less concerned about the shape of the curve and more about its dynamics.

Is this change altering the shape of the curve delivering a more democratic distribution of wealth? Probably not. The discussion is still open but we are learning the Internet is a scale-free network. It has a power law distribution and a preferential attachment attribute that leads to a richer-gets-richer dynamics. Prof. Elberse's data shows exactly this. (see more about this on chapter seven)

So, should we invest in the long tail? (Meaning the obscure products in the digital shelf?)

Of course, we should:

- If we are Amazon, we are getting 25% of our revenue from there. It does not mean we will forget the hits we have, but for sure we want to add those 25%.

- If we are a seller with no access to a physical channel, this is probably the only option we have.

- If we are a consumer looking for a niche product maybe this is the only place where we will find it.

- And if we are a manufacturer, for sure we want to keep an eye on our successful products but we would do better understanding the dynamics of the tail – what are the trends, what is being promoted, what defines the speed of such promotions – keeping in mind that most hits need to open their way through the tail before becoming a hit.

We should be less concerned about the shape of the curve – how many are at the top or at the bottom – and more concerned about the dynamics of it – how fast and why titles move from the bottom to the top and vice versa. (see chapter seven – A Scale-free World, for Good or for Bad?)

2. Information Goods
– The democratization of the means of distribution
+ The digital trial and the digital delivery.

So now anyone can have easy access to consumers. The Internet became a gigantic virtual shelf with all kind of products and services for consumers to choose. The Internet democratized the offering. But while this virtual shelf can display the offerings in a way more democratic than before because of physical shelves space limitations, it still can't deliver the physical product, nor allow consumers to feel it or try it.

However, if you are dealing with information goods – sounds, texts, images and videos – the virtual shelf can go beyond the offering. It can also allow consumers to try the goods. And it can deliver those goods almost instantaneously through the IP pipeline with no need for setting up physical supply chains.

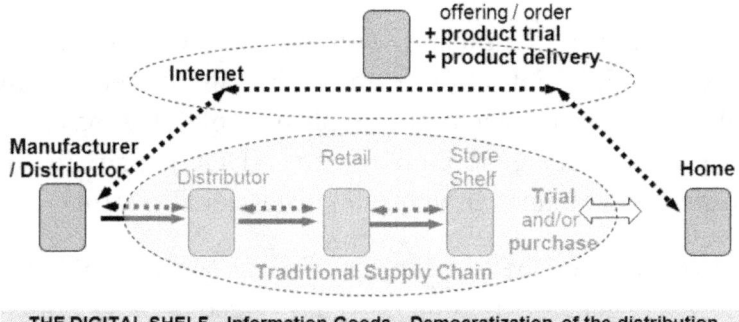

Figure 32: The Digital Shelf – Reshaping the Supply Chain
Information Goods – Democratization of the distribution

Once you add these functionalities to the digital shelf its appeal increases significantly and very little is left to the physical shelves. In such cases there are significant incentives to convert the whole supply chain to the digital channel.

It took some time, but the big labels in the music industry, now understand this. But others understood it first. And they had no legacy issues or old stream of revenues to protect. While Dell and Amazon.com built a "**hybrid digital shelf**" separating product offerings from physical delivery, Apple could build a "**full digital shelf**" in the music arena. Consumers could then shop through a huge assortment of music. And they could try it, buy it, and have it delivered at the moment they closed the purchase.[193]

---

[193] Amazon is now adopting a "full digital shelf" strategy in his bookstore section with the Kindler initiative, which allow people have full access to books with no need to buy the physical product.

3. Information Goods
– The Democratization of the means of production
– The UGC (user-generated content) explosion
– An era of cultural richness and abundant choice

Word processing, publishing software, low cost digital still cameras, high definition camcorders and video editing software have triggered the explosion of what has been called the user-generated-content (UGC) and to the proliferation of amateur and semiprofessional creators.

In a report published in June 2007 Bear Stearns calculates that user generated content (e.g.: videos, blogs, social networks, etc.) already accounted for at least 13% of Internet traffic with a steady month after month growth.[194]

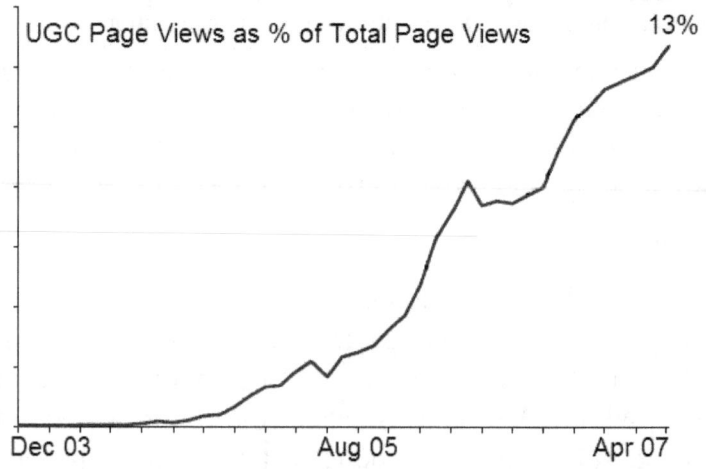

Figure 33: UGC growth **(Wang, Mukherjee, & Anninger, 2007)**

---

[194] See "Entertainment Industry: A Longer Look at the Long Tail," at bearstearns.com (Wang, Mukherjee, & Anninger, 2007). The study considers as UGC the page views from the sites: Youtube, Facebook, Myspace, Wikipedia, Blogger and Digg. We could argue much content in these sites are professionally created. In the other hand they don't add a lot of amateur content from other sites like Flickr. So, look at these numbers with caution, just as reference.

Beyond its explosive growth, UGC also shows at the top of consumers' preference. In a Bearn Stearns online video survey, consumers where asked: "What types of videos do you like to watch?" "UGC ranked surprisingly high, as the second most popular content category across all respondents."[195]

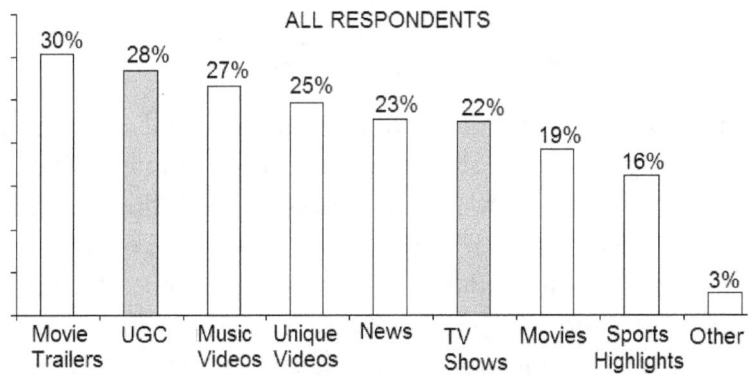

Figure 34: Most popular content category among all survey respondents
(Wang, Mukherjee, & Anninger, 2007)

Among men from 18 to 34 years old UGC ranked number one preference, leaving behind most of the professional video content provided by the incumbent Hollywood studios, TV stations and independent producers:

---

[195] Ibid. (Wang, Mukherjee, & Anninger, 2007)

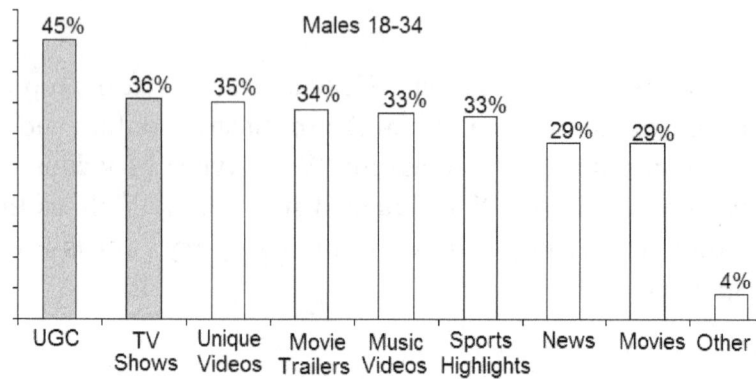

Figure 35: Preferred content category among males 18 to 34 years old
(Wang, Mukherjee, & Anninger, 2007)

This survey shows that these traditional content creators are also losing ground in their relation with consumers. The top three preferred methods for accessing and finding video content were: search engines, forwarded content, and centralized video sites, such as YouTube. *"What is somewhat troubling for media companies is that going to specific TV channels or movie Web sites (like ABC.com or MTV.com) ranked relatively low."* [196]

Bear Stearns perspective is useful to illustrate the relevance of user generated content but it is somehow unfair with professional content because it breaks it apart in different categories. In another study by Pew International published in July 2007 consumers were asked about their preference on professional content – as a whole – against amateur content. They found out the preference for amateur content was higher among young males 18-29 years old: 43% preferred professionally produced videos, versus 34% preferred amateur created and 19% preferred both. For the

---

[196] Ibid. (Wang, Mukherjee, & Anninger, 2007)

general population professional content won 62% versus 19% for amateur versus 11% for both.[197] So, in general terms, and when it is seen as a block, professional content is the one preferred by consumers. Nevertheless user generated content has conquered a significant space.

Other findings of that survey:

- Online video is becoming mainstream:
  - ▸ 74% of broadband users watch or download videos online;
  - ▸ 76% of all young adults (18-29 years old).
- Online surfing is becoming more social. The picture of the lonely internet user buried on his or her computer didn't emerge:
  - ▸ Most online video viewers have watched with other people
  - ▸ More than half of online video viewers share links to the video they find.

As Internet matures and broadband becomes widespread, there is a fundamental change taking placeg. *"Broadband is an integrative activity taking place within the conversations and rhythms of the day,"* says Jeffrey Cole, director of USC's Annenberg School Center for the Digital Future. Cole and his colleagues saw a marked change with the adoption of broadband. *"People started moving their computers into places like the kitchen and family room -- the hubs of home activity."* [198]

---

[197] See "Online Videos Go Mainstream" report by Mary Madden, Jul'07 at pewresearch.org (Madden, 2007)

[198] See "Welcome to My World : It's the consumer's media universe -- you just market in it," Nov'08, by Noreen O'Leary at adweek.com (O'Leary, 2008)

With the democratization of the means of production, the Internet became a legitimate two-way pipeline and people are not just taking stuff out of it as they were supposed to do with the old mass media pipelines but they are also putting stuff into the network.

The digital technology has overturned the traditional distribution chain for information goods opening a channel where the product cannot just be offered but it also can be tried and be delivered at a negligible cost.

In the place of the old autocratic and restrictive physical shelf anyone has now available a digital shelf where anyone can put an offering, opening up an entire new world of abundant choice.

"We are entering an era of Cambrian explosion of creativity… cultural richness and abundant choice we've never seen before in history." [199]

---

[199] Adapted from a statement made by Paul Saffo from the Institute for the Future in the "Among the Audience" survey at Economist.com, (Economist, 2006a)

ELEVEN

Paradox of Choice?

In this chapter we challenge the idea championed by Prof. Barry Schwartz in his book "The Paradox of Choice: Why More is Less," which states that American society has long passed the point "at which increased choice brings misery rather than increased opportunity." We take a look at alternative perspectives on the issue and elaborate on the implications to internet sites, search engines, aggregation models, filtering, recommendation and people participation, relating them to the end of the average-mass mindset.

Indeed, a point is reached at which increased choice brings increased misery rather than increased opportunity. It appears that American society has long since passed that point.

See "The Tyranny of Choice" by Barry Schwartz, Apr'04, Scientific American (Schwartz, 2004)

The findings from this study show that an extensive array of options can at first seem highly appealing to consumers, yet can reduce their subsequent motivation to purchase the product. Even though consumers presumably shop at this particular store in part because of the large number of selections available, having "too much" choice seems nonetheless to have hampered their later motivation to buy.

See "When Choice is Demotivating" (Iyengar & Lepper, 2000)

Prof. Sheena S.Iyengar of Columbia and Mark R.Lepper of Stanford got a remarkable result from an experiment.[200] They set up a table with samples of jams at a specialty food store. After customers tasted as many jams they wanted to taste, these customers got a $1.00 discount to buy any jam they wanted. Half of the time the experiment offered 6 flavors of jams, and half of the time it offered 24 flavors. The striking result: 30% of customers who tasted jams from the small selection bought a jar, while just 3% of those who tasted jams from the bigger selection bought one.

Barry Schwarz – sociology professor at Swarthmore College – in his book: *"The Paradox of Choice, When More is Less,"* develops the idea that too many choices can lead to anxiety, dissatisfaction and regret, making our life worse rather than better.[201] Schwartz argues that too many choices rises our uncertainty and make us uncomfortable with the decisions we make, even before we make them, due to higher expectations, higher risk of regret and higher responsibility – we become the ones to be blamed if we make the wrong choice. He says that in the long run, too many choices can lead to decision-making paralysis, anxiety and even clinical depression.

Schwarz gives us many examples to support his point, some based on research, like the ones done by Iyengar and Lepper, and others based on anecdotal situations, which strike some resonance with most of us.

---

[200] See "When Choice is Demotivating: Can One Desire Too Much of a Good Thing?" (Iyengar & Lepper, 2000)
[201] See Barry Schwarz's video "The Paradox of Choice – Why More is Less" at Google Video (Schwartz, 2006)

Who has never been, at some point, dizzy by too many choices?

Schwartz examples: 285 varieties of cookies at his supermarket, 175 different salad dressings if you don't count the 10 extra virgin olive oils and 12 balsamic vinegars; almost unlimited variety of phones, with too many features.

He tells us his experience when he once went to buy new jeans at The Gap:[202]

> There was a time when jeans came in one flavor, and you bought them, and they fit like crap, and they were incredibly uncomfortable, and if you wore them long enough, and wash them enough times they'd start to fit, fill OK. So I went to replace my jeans after years and years of wearing these old ones and I said I want a pair of jeans, here is my size...
>
> The shopkeeper said: Do you want slim fit, easy fit or relaxed fit? Do you want button-fly or zipper-fly? Stone-washed or acid-washed? Do you want it distressed? ...
>
> My jaw dropped and after I recovered I said: I want the kind that used to be the only kind.
>
> He had no idea what that was, so I spent an hour trying all these different jeans and I walked out of the store, truth, with the best fitting jeans I have ever had. I did

---

[202] Schwartz writes about it in the opening chapter of his book. You can see him talking about it in this shorter presentation at University Web Developers site from which I've made the transcriptions above, or see the original post at TED site. (Schwartz, Paradox of Choice presentation, 2005)

better. All these choices made it possible for me to do better. But, I felt worse.

Why?…with all those options available my expectations about how good a pair of jeans should be, went up. I had very low, no particular expectations when all came in one flavor…

Adding options to people's lives can't help but increase the expectations people have about how good those options will be and these will produce less satisfaction with results, even when they are good results.

One consequence of buying a bad fitting pair of jeans when there is only one kind to buy is that when you are dissatisfied and you ask: Why? Who is responsible? The answer is clear: the world is responsible, what could you do?

When there are hundreds of different styles of jeans available, and you buy one that is disappointing, it is equally clear that the answer to the question is: You. You could have done better.

Barry Schwartz's book had a strong repercussion and many positive reviews, with many people recognizing moments in their lives when they faced some kind of paralysis or dizziness when facing too many choices.

But, let's say we agree that America society has really *"long passed the point at which increased choice brings increased misery rather than increased opportunity."* So should America society leaders take action, limiting the indiscriminate proliferation of choices?

Should the telephone companies eliminate the many options we have today and get back to the time when we simply had one option: the equipment that was automatically sent to our homes at the time of the subscription?

Should the Congress pass a bill determining the maximum variety of cookies, and salad dressings, and cheese, allowed in a supermarket isle? Or, maybe, should the manufacturers agree among themselves to limit the options they should be allowed to launch?

Or, in a lower profile solution, the supermarket store manager should be the one reducing radically the number of options, keeping just a few best sellers in each category, and therefore rescuing the store's consumers from their misery of choosing among too many options?

Let's say the store manager takes the action and reduces the store's assortment to help the store's customers deal with their anxiety when facing too many choices. Probably, as soon as the store manager does it, he or she will get many complaints from the cheese-lovers because they won't be getting all the variety they loved to have.

So the manager will decide to bring the cheese variety back to attend the cheese-lovers demand. Meanwhile, most consumers won't have even noticed the back and forth changes provided the bestseller cheese was kept in the same place all the time.

Next will be the wine-lovers. If consumers actively complain, instead of just moving to a competitor's store, the changes will probably be reverted in all categories. One by one they will turn back to all the variety they had, before the manager decided to do all that simplification. After all, wasn't trying to attend the demand of different groups of people that all that original variety came in place?

If too many choices make consumers feel worse, shouldn't the stores with too many choices be less competitive, giving space to those carrying a reduced set of choices, where consumers would be happier while shopping?

If you ask consumers, you probably won't find one who cares about all the variety in all categories in the whole store, unless he or she is the store manager or a professor doing research on product assortment.

Most people will have a few categories they really care about, where they want plenty of choices, where they like to explore. Or maybe they are just allergic to the top-seller products and need a special one.

Ok, the store manager would say, so let's bring the allergenic products back. But then you have the people that, also for good reasons, need nonfat products, and the kids who need vitamin-enriched products, and the ones that really believe that we should have only organic products. And soon the store manager will bring back the initial huge assortment and will understand that **variety of choices is a way to respect people**. Because real people are not averages[203] and because one-size-fits-all doesn't respect individualities.

Prof. S.Iyengar and M.Lepper point out a situation where more choices would do better for the people involved:[204]

---

[203] See chapter seven: A Scale-free world, for Good or for Bad? How the average-thinking got rooted in our minds and how this digital revolution is moving us away from it.

[204] See "When Choice is Demotivating: Can One Desire Too Much of a Good Thing?" (Iyengar & Lepper, 2000)

Certainly, there are cases when even a vast array of choices may still have beneficial effects. Imagine a group of people who arrive at a new restaurant, for example, all hoping to order their personal favorite dishes. Obviously, the more items offered on the menu, the more satisfied these customers will be, on average. More generally, in preference-matching contexts, in which people enter hoping to find some particular product or service they already know themselves to prefer, larger numbers of options should increase the likelihood that they will be successful in their search.

All of us can remember a few situations when we felt uncomfortable with all the choices we had. All of us can sympathize with the problem stated by Prof. Barry Schwartz. But is the paradox of choice a recurrent problem or is it just the exception? Would Prof. Schwartz feel the same way the second, or the third time he goes back to The Gap to buy his jeans? Would the jam experiment have the same results if consumers could repeat it a few times? Or if it was made within a group of jam-lovers?

"In a familiar environment, people aren't overwhelmed by choice. With experience, we learn to negotiate the alternatives. Schwartz may have trouble in The Gap, but a teenager who owns nine pairs of jeans doesn't. As Schwartz himself notes, 'A small-town resident who visits Manhattan is overwhelmed by all that is going on. A New Yorker, thoroughly adapted to the city's hyperstimulation, is oblivious to it.'"[205]

---

[205] See the excellent article "Consumer Vertigo: A new wave of social critics claim that freedom's just another word for way too much to choose. Here's why they're wrong" by Virginia Postrel at reason.com (Postrel, 2005)

If we are in a familiar environment, we are comfortable. We make the choices ourselves; we lead. If we are adventuring in new areas, we look for guidance: an expert, a friend, or we just follow the mob. This is how we have been dealing with choices for thousands of years. New Yorkers would be also overwhelmed by choices if they were suddenly transported to a prehistoric hunter-gatherer society.

Maybe for a period in history – during the mass-print-culture era – we had people making the choices for us while we were passively seated in front of our TV. But this didn't make us happier.

Ruut Veenhoven professor of 'social conditions for human happiness' at Erasmus University of Rotterdam in the Netherlands, points out that Schwartz's claim that the increase in choice made life less satisfying – supported by Robert E. Lane's work: "The loss of happiness in market democracies'" – is wrong. "*Average happiness has gone up in most developed nations over the last 30 years,*" says Prof. Veenhoven, "*It is true that happiness has not risen in the USA, but happiness has also not declined in this nation, while the number of 'happy life years' has increased steadily in the USA.*" [206]

We all learn quite rapidly how to reduce our choices to the sets that really matter for us. If you are among those who really like wines, you will be glad to spend some time searching and learning through a very big selection. If you are a jam expert, you probably will be delighted to sample among 100 different flavors of jam.

---

[206] See "Happiness in Multiple Choice Society" by R.Veenhoven, in: Journal of Happiness Studies, 2005, vol. 6, pp. 93-96 or at (Veenhoven, 2005)

This is the beauty of the new world and its "digital shelf." (see chapter ten – The Digital Shelf). Now the choices are made for us, with our participation; not anymore for the fictitious average person targeted by the mass merchants and the mass communicators. The control is shifting from the author and editor's hands, or from the manufacturer and retailer's hands, to the people's – former consumers – hands. In the digital shelf, choice-set (or assortment) reduction is not retailer business. It is our business. We control. We pull. We take responsibility. They can help us, if we ask, but they should define a choice-set for each one of us, not a typical choice-set for the average-consumer.

> " Google doesn't push. They invite us to pull. They don't force on us a set of choices, crowded in a busy page.

A cluttered page on the Internet makes us feel uncomfortable not because it is providing us too many choices, but because it is pushing its own selection of choices on us. Google is probably the best example of a company in this new era that understands this. They don't push; they invite us to pull. They don't force on us an authoritative and limited set of choices, crowded in a busy page. Instead, they open a world of unlimited choices for us, presenting it in a calm mostly white page.

So, what do consumers want see displayed on the digital shelf?

Portals, search engines, social networks, ratings, rankings, recommendations, semantic analysis, experts' reviews, collaborative intelligence, etc., all are different approaches on how to get the right choices in front of a consumer and doing so, get his or her attention.

Much debate is going on about which aggregation model works better and how Internet landscape will look like in the future. Will it be dominated by a search engine like Google, or by a social network like MySpace or Facebook? What will be the role of generic gateways to the web, like Yahoo and AOL portals? Which is the strongest aggregation approach: vertical (with focus on specialized communities or areas of interest) like Expedia (travel) and Zillow (real estate) or horizontal (go across different niches or areas of interest) like YouTube, or even aggregate-the-aggregators like NetVibes and iGoogle? What works better on helping consumers make their choices as they surf the web?

Many times we try to answer the question still having in mind the old mass culture mindset, increasing our chances to get the wrong answer. We need to internalize that the time of one-size-fits-all is over. The time of authorial-authority-I-create-you-consume is over. If we are trying to define this digital shelf assortment ourselves and then display it for consumers' admiration, we have a big chance to get it wrong – even if we do it based on solid consumer research. The average-consumer is dead. We've just entered the era of participation, many-to-many, collaborative creation. The most we allow consumers to build their own shelves, most successful the result will be.

In this new era, the one-to-many and author-to-audience model is being replaced by a many-to-many and everybody-is-author-and-audience-at-the-same-time community model.

People – not consumers – are in the driver's seat. We can invite them, but they are the ones who decide when and how they drive their focus and attention to what they need.

The scarcity has shifted to the middle of the supply chain. In the past content was scarce. Physical shelf space was scarce. Consumers had more attention available than choices. Now, with the democratization of the means of production and the multiplicity of choices at the digital shelf, people's attention became scarce.

> Content creation is approaching commodity status, while platforms that can effectively aggregate content and allocate scarce consumer attention can unlock immense value in the new media marketplace.
>
> See "The Great Media Industry" by Scott Karp,   Feb'07 at publishing2.com

> Look at the businesses that have scaled — Google, MySpace, YouTube — all platforms for content, but not producers of content...Even portals like AOL and Yahoo are much more aggregators of content than original producers of content.
>
> See "Content Business Don't Scale Anymore" by Scott Karp, Dec'06 at publishing2.com

The old model was *"based on aggregating large passive audiences and holding them captive during advertising interruptions."* [207] *In the new model, audiences are active and their boundaries with creators are becoming blurred. The way they interact with their choices became critical. They don't just consume what is available in the digital shelf, but now they participate on its creation.*

---

[207] See "Among the Audience," (Economist, 2006a)

People can interact with this digital shelf in different ways, as they do in their life when facing multiple choices.

If they are in a familiar environment, if they feel comfortable, they will probably prefer to make the choices themselves, they will lead. They will probably have pleasure looking for shelves with plenty of choices, searching for that old book, that special music, that documentary that only a few like them have interest in their city. They will build communities around that topic, they will become experts, and they will collaborate creating even more choices, creating user-generated-content, which they will put on the digital shelf themselves.

> " People don't just consume what is available in the digital shelf. Now they participate on its creation.

If they are adventuring in new areas, they will probably look for guidance. They can search for someone in their social network: a friend or an expert and ask for a limited set of choices or for a recommendation. The expert (who probably is part of an experts' community) can be a person, a brand or a site that has built a good reputation around that topic. Another option will be simply to go with the crowd. Check what the crowd is doing, what they are reading, listening, watching or using and try some of the same. But not every crowd. If in a specific context I am a zebra, I will be better running with the other zebras, not with the lions. So social networks and different communities around different topics will help people navigate through a world of unlimited choices (as they already do in the physical world).

The theory of scale-free networks reflects this kind of build up: stronger ties forming clusters or communities, which can specialize in specific topics, and weaker ties connecting across communities in a fractal growth. People most of the time are revolving around one or a few focal clusters (or communities). When they need to face choices beyond their comfort zone, beyond their regular communities, they search for a hub within their network that can link them to another community, which will provide the guidance on the unusual choices they need to make.

As the digital shelf comes to replace or complement the retailers' physical shelves, brands, communities and social networks assume a very important role in the process. Retailers are agents of trust. Consumers have ongoing relationships established with retailers. They know they can return an item if it doesn't work as expected. They know they can give their credit card and other personal information without risk. Manufacturers also have ongoing relationships with retailers. They know they will be paid for the products delivered.

At first Internet was about anarchy, about *"anonymity, playing with your own identity and messing with other people's head,"*[208] but this is changing fast and social networks like Facebook are spearheading these changes. They are bringing, or reinforcing, elements of transparency, trust and reputations into the World Wide Web environment, which are critical to lubricate relationships and allow business and commercial transactions to happen. Social networks are one additional step on our way back towards the old villages (see the chapter three - Back to the Village) where reputations were incredibly important determining

---

[208] Take a look at "Why Facebook Is the Future," by Lev Grossman, Aug'07 at time.com (Grossman, 2007)

people's ability to buy or to sell and to develop all benefits of reciprocal respect.

Who hasn't used a friend to get a job or to figure out what movie to see? Our social networks are now being turbocharged by the digital technology. People will increasingly refer to their online communities and their online social networks when making their choices, balancing their options and gauging brands, sites and people reputations.

"We are entering an era of Cambrian explosion of creativity... cultural richness and abundant choice we've never seen before in history." [209]

And our life has a good chance to get better, because without the need to force ourselves within a fictitious average one-size-fits-all mold, we will have a better chance to find out what's right for each one of us.

Electronic music pioneer Thomas Dolby said:[210] *"As a musician, I'm delighted with the way things are going. I actually think it is a great time for music, because all of these conventions are breaking down. I'm conscious that every song I write now will be around forever (on the Internet) and doesn't have to be part of a co-ordinated marketing campaign – or an album. The Internet is the best of both worlds.* **I can record and release a song, and – a month later – if I don't like a verse, I can change it."**

(My highlight. See the epilogue: "The Breathing Mesh.")

---

[209] Adapted from a statement made by Paul Saffo from the Institute for the Future in the "Among the Audience" (Economist, 2006a)
[210] See "Vanishing Act" by George Varga (San Diego Union Tribune), (Varga, 2006)

The Breathing Mesh

In this chapter we close the loop getting back to the core purpose of the whole book (and website). It puts in contrast the old literate-mass-media and the new hyper-oral-participative paradigms. It highlights how the focus on the individual is changing back to the collective as we move "back to the old village." The mindset is changing. Instead of an individual hero taking care of the whole, the model is about millions of people, each one taking care of small pieces. The pre-packed, pre-thought, one-way content is giving room back to services and evanescent experiences. Top-down-hierarchical-intelligent-design approach is giving way to bottom-up-sprouting-order. A new kind of life is emerging from the mesh.

As a musician, I'm delighted with the way things are going... The Internet is the best of both worlds. I can record and release a song, and – a month later – if I don't like a verse, I can change it.

See "Vanishing Act" (Varga, 2006)

Once we connected those media ponds scattered all over the place and opened the dams allowing free multiple-way flows, a subtle but powerful transformation started to happen – the mesh started to breathe. It became alive. Then, the live event broke out of the frozen content shell, releasing the shadows. And the people were thrown back into the stream – from which they had been kept apart for so long. Passive consumption gave way to collaborative creation. One-way I-talk-you-listen lectures gave way to multiple-way rich conversations. I-tell-you-the-facts-you-just-listen authorial authority of closed pretense truths gave way to live debates and ever changing collective interpretations. People were, once again, living the show, not just watching the shadows projected on the wall. They were drinking at the stream directly connected to the whole, living the moment, together, within the breathing mesh.[211]

. . .

At the 2008 SXSW Interactive conference in Austin, Texas, a turbulent interview stole the show, becoming the conference's big story. Sarah Lacy, a Business Week columnist, was interviewing Mark Zuckerberg, the Facebook founder and CEO.

It could have been just one more among many dull interviews, where part of the audience feel asleep and the other part simply leaves the room in search of a more interesting subject. But this audience didn't do any of that. They started messaging – or in this case, twittering [212] – each other. Suddenly there was, in that room, an instantly

---

[211] Excerpt from the Prologue: "A Tale About the Shadows"

[212] "twittering" refers to using Twitter to exchange short messages with a group of people – See twitter.com

formed community sharing their disgust about what was happening on the stage. Realizing their individual objections were held collectively, they started to voice their displeasure: "Ask him something interesting…"   "Let us ask questions…"

Dan Fost writes about it:[213]

> …finally, when she opened the mike to questions, the first person asked Zuckerberg:"Other than rough interviews, what are some of the biggest challenges Facebook faces?" Lacy turned to Zuckerberg, asked, "Has this been a rough interview?" and the audience member said, "I wasn't asking you, I was asking Mark." The crowd went wild.
>
> A bitter Lacy said she saw in the debacle "the downside of Web 2.0," but many others see it as a signature moment – for what it says about the coming wave of new media, for what it says about the way attendees can take over conferences, and even for the signals it sends about the still rising tide of people power that Web 2.0 has unleashed.

Much has been discussed about this interview. Many of Lacy's mistakes were listed. Among them:[214]

- She didn't care to know about her audience so she focused on her area of interest, asking business questions, while the audience was interested in technology and society.

---

[213] See "Welcome to Conference 2.0" by Dan Fost, Mar'08 at money.cnn.com (Fost, 2008)

[214] Probably the best analysis is at :"Zuckerberg interview: What went wrong." by Jeff Jarvis, Mar'08 at buzzmachine.com (Jarvis, 2008)

- She condescended to him, indirectly affecting the audience.
- She interrupted him and she pre-empted him.
- She inserted herself too much into the interview, telling her stories and giving her opinions up to the point Zuckergerg asked her if she wasn't supposed to ask him a question.
- Probably trying to make him more comfortable, her posture became too friendly and less professional.

As people debated about the interview, many came on Lacy's defense condemning the audience behavior: *"Instead of heckling, people should get up and leave."*

But isn't "get up and leave" what we do when we don't like a TV show? Isn't this thought, part of the old literate-mass-media paradigm when passive audiences had no way to participate, no way to change the outcome of a pre-packed one-way-delivered content?

As we try to better understand what happened that day, it comes clear that it was a clash between the old mass printing culture paradigm and the new participative media era. Beyond the listed mistakes, Sarah Lacy tried to drive the interview in the old style, where she was supposed to control, and the audience to be controlled. Where the people at the stage were supposed to talk and the people at the floor were supposed to stay quiet and listen. Where she was supposed to create and deliver, while the audience should consume. Twittering was out of her equation. And like in the old world, her agenda was static. She had a plan about what she wanted to deliver and she wasn't able to dynamically adjust this plan despite the signs coming from the crowd, up to the point where she totally lost the audience.

And she kept locked into the old mass culture paradigm as Jeff Jarvis points out:[215]

> ...at the end, when she said that people should send her an email telling her what went wrong, she was so 1994; she didn't understand that the people in the crowd were already coalescing in Twitter and blogs into an instant consensus. Oh, if only there'd been a back-channel chat projected on the screen beside her. Then, she could have seen.
>
> After it was over, Lacy did go to Twitter and left this message: "in my book, getting Mark to publicly admit to the Yahoo deal, address Beacon, and give news on changes in the platform and France, equals successful interview." [These were hot topics that she was able to get Mark to talk about]

Lacy was possibly right from old media, literate society standpoint. If her interview was to be written, it could have been a good one. But it was alive, and Lacy was facing an audience very different from the old mass culture people. She was facing an audience composed mainly of digital natives at the edge of the digital technology. They were on top of their social network having key information – including audience mood – being mapped real-time in their twitter radar screen;[216] while she was disconnected. And worst of all, she was trying to deliver them content, a closed one-way product; but they didn't want a one-way delivery,

---

[215] Ibid.

[216] See the Preface: "Writing a Book about the End of Books"

they wanted a service. They wanted an open event rather than a "contained" content. They wanted a multiple-way participative conversation.

> **❝She was trying to deliver them content, a closed one-way product; but they didn't want a one-way delivery, they wanted a participative conversation.**

Her opinion about the interview outcome reflects the one-way mass culture mindset, which presupposes distance between author and reader. One more time she was trying to "deliver" her "one-way" judgment, from-her-to-the-audience, *"NYTimes-like, telling them what the story really was, not the one they saw."* [217]

But in this new world the authority has reverted to the people as Jennifer Laycock asserts: *"Ultimately, it doesn't matter if YOU think you screwed up. If the audience thinks you screwed up, you did. Their perception becomes your reality."* [218]

SXSW conference was packed with digital natives riding the top of the wave of digital technology. The clash between speakers and audience got more visible in Zuckerberg's interview but it wasn't the only place where it happened. In another room where things were not working well, from the audience perspective, *"one person finally stood and requested permission to ask a question. They said 'No'. He said, 'The whole room is behind me.* [he knew it through the web] *I'm going to ask it anyway'."* [219]

---

[217] See "Zuckerberg interview: What went wrong." by Jeff Jarvis, Mar'08 at buzzmachine.com (Jarvis, 2008)
[218] See "Four Social Media Lessons from SXSW" by Jennifer Laycock, Mar'08 (Laycock, 2008)
[219] See "Welcome to Conference 2.0" (Fost, 2008)

Lewis Wallace writes:[220]

> ...it became clear that the fuzzy distinction between the speakers and audience is gone in both the real and virtual worlds... While it might be a rough time to be a speaker, it's a great time to be an attendee...There's a whole new level of interactivity here. At the very essence, what we're about here is conversations. Whether it's a conversation that starts in a panel or from meeting someone at a party.

SXSW clashes are the tip of the iceberg. They highlight the tension building up within our society as we head back to the old oral societies model.[221] Now, with

" While it might be a rough time to be a speaker, it's a great time to be an attendee.

the power of the digital medium, we are becoming hyper-oral. Ong [222] called to our attention that oral societies are agonistically toned. This came out clear from SXSW digital-natives audience combative style. Other characteristics can also be fairly related to the clash between new generation audience and their old mass-culture speakers:[223]

---

[220] See "SXSW" by Lewis Wallace, Mar'08 at blog.wired.com (Wallace, 2008)

[221] See the chapter three "Back to the Village"

[222] See the chapter two "Changing Media, Changing Us"

[223] The table in the next page states some paradigm shifts when we moved from oral to literate societies and now to a hyper-oral society. Take a look at chapter three "Back to the Village"

BACK TO THE VILLAGE

Oral Societies		Literate Societies		Hyper-oral Societies	
Ever changing thought	vs.	Feeling of Closure	vs.	Back to Conversation	Blogs, forums, wikis and fluid flow of information through links and hypertext.
Evanescent Event	vs.	Boxed Content	vs.	Ever changing experience	Content gives way to services, debates, dynamic real time mash ups.
Collective Creation	vs.	Authorial authority	vs.	Collective Creation	Open source, wikis, mash ups, collaboration, create on the go depending on each participant action
Group of Listener	vs.	Lonely Reader	vs.	Online Communities	Forums, chat rooms, IM, Twitter, Social Networks
Pragmatic, Empathetic Participation	vs.	Individual Abstraction	vs.	Communal Participation	New civic sphere where people build ad-hoc communities. Pragmatic. Bottom up surveillance.
Aggregative, Redundant, non-hierarchical thought	vs.	Analytical, Linear and Hierarchical thought	vs.	Aggregative, Parallel, Networked thought	Mash ups, Hyperlink jumps, collaborative creations, collective interpretations.
Conservative and Agonistically toned	vs.	Investigative and Conciliatory	vs.	Engagement	Back to personal debates and struggles, but without memory limitations

Table 7: Back to the Village – from Oral to Literate to Hyper-oral

Not just conflicts but also good results came out of the high level of connectivity and interactivity of SXSW attendees. In more than one panel, discussions were actively turned into a better direction, producing better outcomes to all participants, when speakers and audience could engage in a more participative mode.

Ripples of Zuckerberg's interview spread through the Web generating a remarkable debate. Many different and relevant points of view were stated. Some defending Sarah Lacy saying she did a great interview under the hostile circumstances.[224] Others commenting on the rudeness of the mob and their lack of civility. Tom Davenport wrote on Harvard Business Online, "Could Twitter threaten free speech?" [225]

> This idea that you should Twitter about the speaker or interviewer while they are speaking at a conference is an interesting and increasingly popular one. I certainly wouldn't advocate trying to stop it, but I would encourage potential and actual critical Twitterers to think carefully about where this all goes. You may not like intermediaries between yourself and people like Zuckerberg, but even (presumably) socially oriented folks like him may like a little bit more control than an open dialogue with a crowd would involve...
>
> If the leading thinkers of the world feel that they will be attacked on the back channel, they may not want to play...

---

[224] See "Sarah Lacy on Sarah Lacy and the SXSW Mark Zuckerberg Keynote" by Brian Solis, Mar'08 (Solis, 2008)

[225] See "Could Twitter Threaten Free Speech?" by Tom Davenport, Mar'08 at Harvard Business Publishing. (Davenport, 2008)

> We have to balance the idea of unfettered self-expression with civility. If we're not civil, it will probably lead to less free speech, not more.

But different paradigms can lead to different understanding of civility. The old literate-mass-media paradigm thinks in terms of hierarchy, speech and control while the new hyper-oral paradigm thinks in terms of participative conversation and collaborative creation.

While many outsiders felt that some people in the audience were being rude – and some of them indeed were –, most in the audience felt Sarah Lacy was the rude one, because she was trying to carry her own agenda with no concern about what the audience wanted. She was trying to control them, trying to please them her own way while keeping them at distance.

As it was pointed out, what happened in that interview was a signature moment for a new society that is emerging. We are moving into a new civic sphere where people will not look above them anymore, searching for hierarchies and established institutions to tell them what is the truth and what they are supposed to do. People will, instead, look to each other and define together how to interpret the truth.[226] They will engage on collective creation, on the go, defining their plans to action.

Speakers, interviewers, politicians, CEOs will need to adapt. They will need to understand that in this new world people don't want packed truths and speeches formatted

---

[226] See Jeremiah Owyang talking about "growndswell" at A "Groundswell at SXSW: How the Audience Revolted and Asserted Control" by Jeremiah Owyang, Mar'08 (Owyang, 2008)

like products; people want conversations; they don't want content, they want services and open events. In this new world ME is becoming US. And it will be better to become part of US than keep trying to drive – or sometimes, ride – the ghost of the departed average-consumer.

Metaphors, Ideas and Paradigm Shifts

about understanding new concepts:

about the end of literate-mass-media era:

about the online communication and networking:

In the literate society the world of writing and world of talking weren't supposed to mix with each other, 4

It's not about the content but about the contact, 5

It is a different model. Less contact, with a lot more people, demanding a constant flow of contact, lots of little contacts, just a blip on the screen, just a way of "checking in" (adapted from Grant McCracken ideas), 5

It works like a radar screen, or a sonar screen, where people are constantly "pinging" each other, keeping the links in the network active and the information flowing within their screen, 6

about changing media, changing us:

The medium is the message (Marshal McLuhan), 25, 41

The dominant medium traits rather than its content have the power to shape people's way of thinking and behavior, 41

What is a tree? (Dino Felluga), 26

Feeling of closure vs. ever changing thought – in oral societies ideas and stories were alive, continuously transforming every time they were told or discussed, 31

Boxed content vs. evanescent event – an event cannot be carried around; it simply happens, 32

Authorial authority vs. collective creation – the very idea of authorship and of the ownership of original work is connected to the establishment of literate culture. Copyright is only possible after copywright (Dino Felluga), 33

A lonely reader vs. group of listeners, 34

Individual abstraction vs. pragmatic and empathetic participation – writing presupposes distance in time and space between author and reader (Robert Fowler), 35

Analytical, linear, hierarchical thought vs. aggregative, redundant, non-hierarchical – from the circular world of sound with its round huts and round villages, people move, over time, toward linear, cause-and-effect thinking, grid-like cities, and a one-thing-at-a-time and one-thing-after-another, and take-time-to-think world (Joshua Meyrowitz), 37

Investigative and conciliatory mindset vs. conservative and agonistically toned mindset – writing is more rational, less emotional and more conciliatory. It disengage humans from direct, interpersonal struggle, 38

Digital natives, Digital immigrants (Marc Prensky), 22

about going back to the village:

We see ourselves back to the old village. But it is an old village on steroids, where our memory and our reach have been multiplied manifold, 41, 47

Rather than hierarchical structures and editorial filters we will probably find out what matter most is who the wiki attracts to its community and what is the level of engagement of its members. Because a wiki is nothing more than an expression of its community; an expression of the village, 60

From oral to literate societies, 31

From literate to hyper-oral societies

about participative bottom-up creation vs. top-down authoritative design:

The time of authorial-authority-I-create-you-consume is over. The average-consumer is dead. We've just entered the era of participation, many-to-many, collaborative creation, 188

The old author-thought, one-way, one-to-many hierarchical mass communication flow is giving way to a new collaborative-thought, multiple-ways, many-to-many, networked flow, 48

The old media model was: there is one source of truth. The new media model is: there are multiple sources of truth, and we will sort it out (Joe Kraus), 56

People are looking to their peers – instead of looking for authorities – and decisions and solutions are surfacing from the bottom, 43, 46

The fuzzy distinction between the speakers and audience is gone in both the real and virtual worlds (Lewis Wallace), 199

In this new era, the one-to-many and author-to-audience model is being replaced by a many-to-many and everybody-is-author-and-audience-at-the-same-time community model, 188

Could Twitter threaten free speech?, 201

about the print mold and the mass media era:

The Gutenberg Bible was one of the first mass manufactured products in this world. The paper was the first mass medium. The model, one to many instead of one to one – was much more productive, 62

This has been the model that put incredible machines working for us and raised the standard of living at a level that old villages' people would never be able to imagine, 64

At that point general people had never known so much, and their knowledge had never been so homogeneous, because it was made prisoner of the same mold. People were following, like cattle, the editors' choices and the authors' pretense truths, 65

You had no other option than attach your creation (thoughts, stories, music, text, etc.) to a physical medium before having them distributed to your buyers and consumers. The control was in the hands of the large media companies, 67

about the landgrab fight:

Large media companies' economies of scale, plus the knowledge and investment accumulated on dealing with their medium – paper, vinyl or airwaves – acted like silo walls protecting them from an alien assault, 66

The recording industry couldn't understand the time of heavy-hand control was over and that their silo walls were collapsing, 70

In this new world there are no more exclusive turfs. The land is up for grabs, 74

If you think: "I'm fine, my company is not in the Media Industry," think again. There is a chance you have been already thrown in a fight and you are not even aware of it, 76

about the crumbling advertising mold:

There was a concealed deal in the old advertising model. Consumers could watch a TV show for free provided they watched passively the advertisements inserted in the middle of the show. Advertisers were paying for the show in exchange for consumers' attention at break time, 80

The traditional advertising model requires typical mass consumers who passively watch, or hear, or read the one-way communication that comes to their senses. The model breaks apart when consumers become active, when they take control, skipping advertising, 79

The mass advertising model is very inefficient to most products. Advertisers scream their message to millions of people so just the 1% who needs their product can hear them. For the other 99% the message is noise. And for advertisers, this noise is wasted money, 86

Mass advertisers do not really know whether it is working or not. Traditional advertising requires an expensive act of faith by its buyers because the linkage between the broadcast of an ad and a consumer buying decision is unclear and uncertain (Accenture), 87

The digital natives, raised in the world of video games and cluttered advertising, grew aware of the value of their attention and learned to focus on what mattered to them, 82

Having at their hand multiple resources like laptops, mobile phones, instant messages and SMS, they learned to multitask and selectively drive their attention, discarding instinctively the irrelevant and intrusive advertising messages, 82

People now can avoid becoming hostages of the ad clutter with its widespread screaming. They don't need to surrender to the old push model anymore. Now they can pull, close the loop, participate, and engage in real time conversations, building communities, taking back the control, 92

In the new villages, the people own the point of view. They are the ones deciding who deserves their attention; who gets in or out of their radar screen, 92

People – not consumers – are in the driver's seat. We can invite them, but they are the ones who decide when and how they drive their focus and attention to what they need.

Instead of focus on reach, advertisers should think on how to be easily reached; on how to clean the path and spread the word so people can find them, 93

How far can a company go, trying to insert itself in people's radar before jeopardizing the company's reputation and people's friendships?, 95

If there is still an opportunity to trade people's attention for advertisers' sales pitch, this trade will not go undercover anymore. It won't be a mass deal. It will be a one-on-one negotiation where people understand the value of their attention because they are conscious of its scarcity, 96

about reputation:

At the villages, reputations are built bottom up. You cannot build them through top-down pitches anymore, because people are not any longer sitting passively absorbing the messages coming through the tube, 96

The new village is no longer about monologues. It is about conversations. It is not about consensus, but about debate. It is about understanding the different points of view of every thinker as well as the thinker reputation, 57

In a conversation, not only what is being said matters, but also the reputation of the one who is saying it.

Anonymity is a modern print-mass-culture innovation (adapted from Clive Thompson), 57

Privacy is not an option (Aaron Schmidt), 59

Lack of privacy is not a bug, but a feature of the network (adapted from Aaron Schmidt), 59

about average-thinking:

The literate-mass-media era became the era of the average, 107

We need to free ourselves from average thinking (Philip W. Anderson), 130, 171

Gaussian-mold-reasoning: consumer instead of people, average instead of specific, mass instead of individual.

Most quantitative research involves the use of statistical methods presuming independence among data points, but in the connected world interdependency is predominant (adapted from Andriani & McKelvey), 117

In a scale free world, averages have no meaning, 110,

In a scale free world we must be aware of the outliers as they have more meaning than anything at the mean, 120, 130

Normal distribution and averages can lead to totally flawed reasoning, 110

As many as 80 percent of randomly selected Internet routers can fail and the remaining ones will still form a compact cluster. (Barabasi & Bonabeau), 116

Most of us would expect a rising number of choices to flatten the curve (Clay Shirky), 112

Understanding scale-free networks requires a dynamic view of the landscape, rather than a snapshot of the curve's shape, 120, 128

about innovation speed and wealth:

Throughout history, scientific discoveries and innovations came as a consequence of an interconnected web of knowledge, people and events transcending any closed quarter (adapted from James Burke), 56, 100

Myth of the lonely genius, 55, 100

The ease with which information can be spread is critical to the rate at which change occurs (James Burke), 101, 123

Now we can have the reach and the permanence of the mass mold but with the speed and fluidity of the old conversations, 121

People have a lot more chance now to bubble up. The viscosity of the system has dropped to a large extent., 128

Matching labor demand with supply, 124

The optimists call attention to the potential we have ahead of us and feed creativity. The pessimists call attention to the risks and feed institutional reforms, 131

If the interdependencies and feedback loops in our big scale-free network were good enough to consider properly the risks pointed out by the pessimists, maybe we will be fortunate to have a future that is closer to the optimists dream, 134

about content:

Most of us didn't realize our literate concept of inert "content" is an old paradigm, which has been engraved in our minds through the last 500 years, vii

Information became a package good coughed out by a mold. It lost the speed and fluidity of a local debate where propositions are refuted right away and solutions come out as a result of interaction among the participants. Learning became a solitaire exercise where we read static snapshots of thoughts in a printed book, 106

Writing was an attempt to turn living thoughts dwelling in the human mind into mere objects in the physical world (Wikipedia), 28

boxed content vs. evanescent event, 32

In the past, music was a social event, an experience. You could pay to hear music, but after you did, it was over, gone - a memory. (adapted from David Byrne), 35

Now "I can record and release a song, and – a month later – if I don't like a verse, I can change it." (Thomas Dolby), 192, 194

about the digital shelf:

about choices:

And our life has a good chance to get better, because without the need to force ourselves within a fictitious average one-size-fits-all mold, we will have a better chance to find out what's right for each one of us, 192

A cluttered page in the Internet make us feel uncomfortable not because it is providing us too many choices, but because it is pushing its own selection of choices on us, 187

Google don't push. They invite us to pull. They don't force on us a set of choices, crowded in a busy page. Instead, they open a world of unlimited choices in a calm mostly white page,

about the breathing mesh:

Shadows revolution is about releasing the inert and locked content from the imprisonment imposed by the physical medium, giving it back that freedom of the old village days, throwing it back into a collaborative, ever-changing, living stream, ix

People

Blogs, Websites, Organizations and Brands

Index

Table of Figures

References and Sources

2Spare. (2006, March 28). *TOP 87 Bad Predictions About The Future.* Retrieved April 4, 2009, from 2Spare: http://www.2spare.com/item_50221.aspx

Accenture. (2007). *Facing the digital reality: the path to future high performance in advertising.* Retrieved April 6, 2009, from Accenture: http://www.accenture.com/NR/rdonlyres/0000f4a9/emugkriavilvejmuuzoveksalfytldlv/2007DigitalAdvertisingStudy.pdf

Adamic, L. A. (2000, October 4). *Power-laws, and Pareto - a ranking tutorial.* Retrieved April 6, 2009, from HP Labs: http://www.hpl.hp.com/research/idl/papers/ranking/

Adamic, L. A., & Huberman, B. A. (2002). *Zipf's law and the Internet.* Retrieved April 6, 2009, from HP Labs: http://www.hpl.hp.com/research/idl/papers/ranking/adamicglottometrics.pdf

Alterman, E. (2008, March 31). *Out of Print: The death and life of the American newspaper.* Retrieved April 6, 2009, from The New Yorker: http://www.newyorker.com/reporting/2008/03/31/080331fa_fact_alterman?currentPage=all

Anderson, C. (2004, October). *The Long Tail.* Retrieved April 7, 2009, from Wired: http://www.wired.com/wired/archive/12.10/tail.html

Anderson, C. (2006, July 14). *The Rise and Fall of the Hit.* Retrieved April 6, 2009, from Wired: http://www.wired.com/wired/archive/14.07/longtail.html

Andriani, P., & McKelvey, B. (2006, July). *Beyond Gaussian Averages: Redirecting Management Research Toward Extreme Events and Power Laws.* Retrieved April 6, 2009, from Durham Business School: http://www.dur.ac.uk/resources/dbs/faculty/working-papers/BeyondGaussianAverages19Jun06.pdf

Apple. (2003, April 28). *Apple Launches the iTunes Music Store.* Retrieved April 6, 2009, from Apple Press Releases: http://www.apple.com/pr/library/2003/apr/28musicstore.html

Armour, S. (2005, November 8). *GenY: They have arrived at work with a new attitude.* Retrieved 4 7, 2009, from USA Today: http://www.usatoday.com/money/workplace/2005-11-06-gen-y_x.htm

Arnold, T. (2003, January). *Using the (Juran) Pareto principle: A simple and very useful concept.* Retrieved April 6, 2009, from Newspapers & Technology: http://www.newsandtech.com/issues/2003/01-03/nt/01-03_arnold.htm

Ayiter, E. (2008). *The History of Visual Communication - chapter 5: The Printing Press.* Retrieved April 5, 2009, from citrinitas.com: http://www.citrinitas.com/history_of_viscom/press.html

Baker, S. (2007, December 13). *Google and the Wisdom of Clouds.* Retrieved April 7, 2009, from BusinessWeek: http://www.businessweek.com/magazine/content/07_52/b4064048925836.htm

Bangeman, E. (2008, April 2). *Apple passes Wal-mart, now #1 music retailer in US.* Retrieved April 6, 2009, from ars technica: http://arstechnica.com/apple/news/2008/04/apple-passes-wal-mart-now-1-music-retailer-in-us.ars

Barabasi, A.-L. (2003). *Linked: the new science of networks.* Basic Books.

Barabasi, A.-L., & Bonabeau, E. (2003, May). *Scale-Free Networks.* Retrieved April 6, 2009, from Scientific American: http://www.sciam.com/article.cfm?id=scale-free-networks

BBC. (1998, June 8). *Football trouble brewing for National Grid.* Retrieved April 6, 2009, from BBC News: http://news.bbc.co.uk/1/hi/uk/109355.stm

BBC. (1998, November 12). *Internet sales boost Dell profits.* Retrieved April 7, 2009, from BBC: http://news.bbc.co.uk/2/hi/business/213422.stm

Bellis, M. (n.d.). *The History of Steam Engines.* Retrieved Apr 6, 2009, from About.com: http://inventors.about.com/library/inventors/blsteamengine.htm

Berman, S. J., Battino, B., Shipnuck, L., & Neus, A. (2007). *The end of advertising as we know it.* Retrieved April 6, 2009, from IBM: http://www-03.ibm.com/industries/global/files/media_ibv_advertisingv2.pdf

Berner, R. (2006, May 29). *I Sold It Through the Grapevine.* Retrieved April 6, 2009, from BusinessWeek: http://www.businessweek.com/magazine/content/06_22/b3986060.htm

Bianco, A. (2004, July 12). *The Vanishing Mass Market.* Retrieved April 6, 2009, from BusinessWeek: http://www.businessweek.com/magazine/content/04_28/b3891001_mz001.htm

Bingham, A. (n.d.). *Review of Walter J. Ong's Orality and Literacy.* Retrieved April 5, 2009, from Northern Illinois University: http://www.engl.niu.edu/wac/ong_rvw.html

Bolon, K. (2001, Spring). *The Steam Engine.* Retrieved April 6, 2009, from University of Dayton: http://campus.udayton.edu/~hume/Steam/steam.htm

Boyd, D. (2008, January 10). *Technology and the World of Consumption.* Retrieved April 6, 2009, from Digital Youth Research: http://digitalyouth.ischool.berkeley.edu/node/110

Brain, M. (n.d.). *How Wikis Work.* Retrieved April 6, 2009, from howstuffworks: http://computer.howstuffworks.com/wiki.htm

Bray, T. (2007, November 28). *On Communication.* Retrieved April 5, 2009, from ongoing: http://www.tbray.org/ongoing/When/200x/2007/11/23/Communication

Breen, B. (2007, December 19). *Living in Dell Time.* Retrieved April 7, 2009, from Fast Company: http://www.fastcompany.com/magazine/88/dell.html

Brynjolfsson, E., Hu, Y. ", & Smith, M. D. (2006, June). *From Niches to Riches: The Anatomy of the Long Tail.* Retrieved April 6, 2009, from CarnegieMellon HeinzCollege: http://www.heinz.cmu.edu/~mds/smr.pdf

Brynjolfsson, E., Hu, Y. (., & Smith, M. D. (2006, December 29). *Consumer Surplus in the Digital Economy: Estimating the Value of Increased Product Variety at Online Booksellers*. Retrieved April 7, 2009, from Erik Brynjolfsson page at MIT Center for Digital Business: http://ebusiness.mit.edu/Erik/ConsumerSurplus.pdf

Brynjolfsson, E., Hu, Y. J., & Simester, D. (2007, November). *Goodbye Pareto Principle, Hello Long Tail: The Effect of Search Costs on the Concentration of Product Sales*. Retrieved April 7, 2009, from Social Science Research Network: http://papers.ssrn.com/sol3/papers.cfm?abstract_id=953587

BSG. (2006, May 12). *Predicting UK Future Residential Bandwidth Requirements*. Retrieved April 7, 2009, from Broadband Stakeholder Group UK: http://www.broadbanduk.org/content/view/185/

Bughin, J., Chui, M., & Johnson, B. (2008, June). *The next step in open innovation*. Retrieved April 6, 2009, from The McKinsey Quarterly: http://www.mckinseyquarterly.com/Information_Technology/Networking/next_step_in_open_innovation_2155

Burke, J. (1978). *Connections*. Litle, Brown.

Burke, J. (2000, December 4). *Inventors & Inventions*. Retrieved April 6, 2009, from Time: http://www.time.com/time/magazine/article/0,9171,998681-1,00.html

Business 2000. (2004). *E-Commerce Within Dell and How This New Way of Doing Business is Managed*. Retrieved April 7, 2009, from Business 2000: http://www.business2000.ie/images/pdfs/dell_7th_ed.pdf

Buvat, J., Mehra, P., & Braunschvig, B. (2007, April). *Digital Natives - How Is the Younger Generation Reshaping the Telecom and Media Landscape?* Retrieved April 6, 2009, from Capgemini: http://www.de.capgemini.com/m/de/tl/Digital_Natives.pdf

Byrne, D. (2007, December 18). *David Byrne's Survival Strategies for Emerging Artists — and Megastars*. Retrieved April 7, 2009, from Wired: http://www.wired.com/entertainment/music/magazine/16-01/ff_byrne

Carneiro, R. L. (2000, September 28om). *The transition from quantity to quality: A neglected causal mechanism in accounting for social evolution*. Retrieved April 6, 2009, from Proceedings of the National Academy of Sciences of the United States of America: http://www.pnas.org/content/97/23/12926.full.pdf

Carr, N. (2008, July/August). *Is Google Making Us Stupid?* Retrieved April 7, 2009, from The Atlantic: http://www.theatlantic.com/doc/200807/google

Carr, N. (2008a). *The Big Switch: Rewiring the World, from Edison to Google*. W.W. Norton & Co.

Carr, N. (2007). *The Ignorance of Crowds*. Retrieved April 6, 2009, from strategy+business: http://www.strategy-business.com/media/file/sb47_07204.pdf

Cazabon, C. (n.d.). *Why Wikipedia Can't Work*. Retrieved April 6, 2009, from Piropus Technology: http://pyropus.ca/personal/writings/wikipedia.html

Chartier, D. (2008, May 20). *VoIP joins cellular in eating away at telecom landlines*. Retrieved April 7, 2009, from ars technica: http://arstechnica.com/business/news/2008/05/voip-joins-cellular-in-eating-away-at-telecom-landlines.ars

Cheung, H. (2006, July 14). *Jessica Simpson sings for you with new customized songs* . Retrieved April 6, 2009, from TG Daily: http://www.tgdaily.com/content/view/27555/98/

CNN. (2006, June 22). *Heaven or hell? How will technology shape our future?* Retrieved April 6, 2009, from CNN: http://edition.cnn.com/2006/TECH/science/06/12/introduction/

Cohen, S. M. (2006, March 17). *The Allegory of the Cave*. Retrieved April 4, 2009, from University of Washington: http://faculty.washington.edu/smcohen/320/cave.htm

Colville, G. (n.d.). *Faith comes by Hearing? About Oral Societies*. Retrieved April 5, 2009, from Global Recordings Network: http://globalrecordings.net/article/162

Comcast. (2008, January 8). *Move Over Bells: Comcast Corporation Becomes The Fourth-Largest Phone Service Provider In The U.S.* Retrieved April 7, 2009, from Comcast Press Releases: http://www.comcast.com/About/PressRelease/PressReleaseDetail.ashx?PRID=721

Crain, C. (2007, December 24). *Twilight of The Books*. Retrieved April 4, 2009, from The New Yorker: http://www.newyorker.com/arts/critics/atlarge/2007/12/24/071224crat_atlarge_crain

Davenport, T. (2008, March 11). *Could Twitter Threaten Free Speech?* Retrieved April 7, 2009, from Harvard Business Publishing: http://discussionleader.hbsp.com/davenport/2008/03/twittering_in_the_backchannel.html

Dee, J. (2007, July 1). *All News That's Fit to Print Out*. Retrieved April 6, 2009, from The New York Times: http://www.nytimes.com/2007/07/01/magazine/01WIKIPEDIA-t.html?pagewanted=all

Diamond, J. (2005). *Guns, Germs and Steel*. W.W. Norton & Co.

DirectMarketing. (1989, July 1). *Mail order top 250+*. Retrieved April 7, 2009, from AllBusinesses: http://www.allbusiness.com/marketing/direct-marketing-direct-mail-mailing-lists/106059-1.html

Duryee, T. (2008, October 21). *Earnings Call: Jobs Says iPhone Revs Total $4.6B, Making Apple The Third-Largest Handset Maker*. Retrieved April 6, 2009, from paidContent.org: http://www.paidcontent.org/entry/419-apple-call-jobs-says-iphone-revs-total-46-billion-making-apple-the-thir/

Economist, T. (2006a, April 20). *Among the audience*. Retrieved April 6, 2009, from Economist.com: http://www.economist.com/surveys/displaystory.cfm?story_id=6794156

Economist, T. (2006b, April 20). *Heard on the street*. Retrieved April 6, 2009, from economist.com: http://www.economist.com/surveys/displaystory.cfm?story_id=6794210

Economist, T. (2006d, April 20). *The wiki principle*. Retrieved April 6, 2009, from Economist.com: http://www.economist.com/surveys/displaystory.cfm?story_id=6794228

Economist, T. (2006c, April 20). *What sort of revolution?* Retrieved April 6, 2009, from Economist.com: http://www.economist.com/surveys/displaystory.cfm?story_id=6794256

Econophysics. (2006, July 18). *Tyranny of the Power Law (and Why We Should Become Eclectic)*. Retrieved April 6, 2009, from Econophysics: http://econophysics.blogspot.com/2006/07/tyranny-of-power-law-and-why-we-should.html

Elberse, A. (2008, July/August). *Should You Invest in the Long Tail?* Retrieved April 7, 2009, from Harvard Business Review: http://hbr.harvardbusiness.org/2008/07/should-you-invest-in-the-long-tail/ar/1

Encarta. (2008). *Montgomery Ward*. Retrieved April 7, 2009, from Microsoft Encarta Online Encyclopedia: http://encarta.msn.com/encnet/refpages/RefArticle.aspx?refid=761577779

Engardio, P. (2008, July 3). *Mom-and-Pop Multinationals*. Retrieved April 6, 2009, from BusinessWeek: http://www.businessweek.com/magazine/content/08_28/b4092077027296.htm?chan=search

Fast_Company. (2007, December 18). *Next Time, What Say We Boil a Consultant*. Retrieved April 4, 2009, from Fast Company: http://www.fastcompany.com/magazine/01/frog.html

Felluga, D. (2003, November 28). *General Introduction to Postmodernism*. Retrieved April 4, 2009, from Introductory Guide to Critical Theory: http://www.cla.purdue.edu/academic/engl/theory/postmodernism/modules/introduction.html

Ferris, S. P. (2002, August). *Writing Electronically: The Effects of Computers on Traditional Writing*. Retrieved December 12, 2008, from The Journal of Electronic Publishing: http://www.press.umich.edu/jep/08-01/ferris.html

Fisher, S. (2008, July 26). *Finding common ground with your kids*. Retrieved April 4, 2009, from Vail Daily: http://www.vaildaily.com/article/20080726/AE/568809160/1064

Fost, D. (2008, March 11). *Welcome to Conference 2.0*. Retrieved April 7, 2009, from CNN Money: http://money.cnn.com/2008/03/11/technology/fost_conference.fortune/?postversion=2008031115

Fowler, R. (1994, November 19). *How the Secondary Orality of the Electronic Age Can Awaken Us to the Primary Orality of Antiquity*. Retrieved April 6, 2009, from Bob Fowler's Publications: http://homepages.bw.edu/~rfowler/pubs/secondoral/index.html

Frazier, M. (2007, January 10). *Information Generation*. Retrieved April 4, 2009, from Mark Proffitt: http://www.markproffitt.com/2007/01/10/43/

Friedman, T. L. (2005, April 3). *It's a Flat World, After All*. Retrieved April 4, 2009, from The New York Times: http://www.nytimes.com/2005/04/03/magazine/03DOMINANCE.html?_r=4&oref=slogin&oref=slogin

Gabriel, M. (2007, October 30). *Apple has destroyed the music business.* Retrieved April 6, 2009, from Antitrust Review: http:// www.antitrustreview.com/archives/1211

GigaOM. (2009, March 11). *Comcast is Now 3rd Largest U.S. Phone Company.* Retrieved April 6, 2009, from GigaOM: http://gigaom.com/2009/03/11/ comcast-is-now-3rd-largest-us-phone-company/

Goldman, A. (2009, July 28). *VoIP Ranking by Subscriber: Q1 2008.* Retrieved April 7, 2009, from ISP Planet: http://www.isp-planet.com/research/rankings/ 2008/voip+q12008.html

Greenberg, A. (2009, March 3). *By The Numbers: Most Influential Twitterers.* Retrieved April 4, 2009, from Forbes: http://www.forbes.com/2009/01/29/top-twitters-celebrities-technology-webceleb09_0129_top_twitters_slide_2.html? thisSpeed=15000

Greene, M. (2002, February 27). *Grammy Speech.* Retrieved April 6, 2009, from Boycott-RIAA: http://www.boycott-riaa.com/education/grammy_speech

Griscom, A. (1996). *Trends of Anarchy and Hierarchy: Comparing the Cultural Repercussions of Print and Digital Media.* Retrieved April 5, 2009, from cyberartsweb.org.

Gross, D. (2008, July 25). *Phones Without Homes, What's really killing the land-line telephone business.* Retrieved April 7, 2009, from Slate: http:// www.slate.com/id/2195765/

Grossman, L. (2007, August 23). *Why Facebook Is the Future.* Retrieved April 7, 2009, from Time: http://www.time.com/time/magazine/article/ 0,9171,1655722,00.html

Hagel, J. (2007, May 2). *The Power of Power Laws.* Retrieved April 6, 2009, from Edges Perspectivies with John Hagel: http:// edgeperspectives.typepad.com/edge_perspectives/2007/05/ the_power_of_po.html

Hanna, J. (2007, September 17). *Broadband: Remaking the Advertising Industry.* Retrieved April 6, 2009, from HBS Working Knowledge: http:// hbswk.hbs.edu/item/5652.html

Harnad, S. (1991). *Post-Gutenberg Galaxy: The Fourth Revolution in the Means of Production of Knowledge.* Retrieved April 4, 2009, from University of Southampton: http://eprints.ecs.soton.ac.uk/3376/2/ harnad91.postgutenberg.html

Holt, R. a. (2000). World History, People and Nations, Ancient World. Housepricecrash. (n.d.). *Housepricecrash.co.uk.* Retrieved April 5, 2009, from What is 'boiled frog syndrome'?: http://www.housepricecrash.co.uk/FAQ-what-is-boiled-frog-syndrome.php

Hume, M. (2007, October 26). *Ten days that shook the world.* Retrieved April 4, 2009, from Spiked: http://www.spiked-online.com/index.php?/site/ reviewofbooks_article/4000/

Iyengar, S. S., & Lepper, M. R. (2000). *When Choice is Demotivating: Can One Desire Too Much of a Good Thing?* Retrieved April 7, 2009, from Prof. Iyengar page at Columbia University: http://www.columbia.edu/~ss957/articles/ Choice_is_Demotivating.pdf

Jarvis, J. (2006, August 14). *Is writing the highest form of speech?* Retrieved April 5, 2009, from Buzzmachine: http://www.buzzmachine.com/2006/08/14/is-writing-the-highest-form-of-speech/

Jarvis, J. (2008, Mar 10). *Zuckerberg interview: What went wrong.* Retrieved April 7, 2009, from BuzzMachine: http://www.buzzmachine.com/2008/03/10/ zuckerberg-interview-what-went-wrong/

Kawasaki, G. (2006, September). *Is Advertising Dead?* Retrieved April 4, 2009, from How to Change the World: http://blog.guykawasaki.com/2006/09/ is_advertising_.html

KEYETV. (2007, September 12). *Internet Allows Bands To Be Seen And Heard.* Retrieved April 7, 2009, from keyetv.com: http://www.keyetv.com/content/ entertainment/austinmusic/story/Internet-Allows-Bands-To-Be-Seen-And-Heard/sE4TSZy5VUCL1tCT6J6R9w.cspx#Scene_1

Kharif, O. (2008, April 14). *Bypassing Carriers for Mobile Content.* Retrieved April 6, 2009, from BusinessWeek: http://www.businessweek.com/technology/ content/apr2008/tc20080414_287344.htm?chan=technology_technology+index +page_top+stories

Kharif, O. (2008a, August 26). *VoIP Goes Mobile.* Retrieved April 6, 2009, from BusinessWeek: http://www.businessweek.com/technology/content/ aug2008/tc20080825_613129.htm

King, R. (2008, August 4). *How Cloud Computing Is Changing the World.* Retrieved April 7, 2009, from BusinessWeek: http://www.businessweek.com/ technology/content/aug2008/tc2008082_445669.htm

King, R. (2007, March 12). *Rest for the Wiki.* Retrieved April 6, 2009, from BusinessWeek: http://www.businessweek.com/technology/content/mar2007/ tc20070312_740461.htm

Kornhaber, D. (1999, February). *Read Between the Lines - Book superstores threaten the American literary future.* Retrieved April 7, 2009, from Harvard Digitas: http://www.digitas.harvard.edu/~perspy/old/issues/1999/feb/read.shtml

Lawrence, M. (2005, September 9). *Statistics Part 1: Average and Standard Deviation.* Retrieved April 6, 2009, from Investing Money: http:// investing.calsci.com/statistics.html

Laycock, J. (2008, March 10). *Four Social Media Lessons from SXSW's Mark Zuckerberg Interview.* Retrieved April 7, 2009, from Search Engine Guide: http://www.searchengineguide.com/jennifer-laycock/four-social-media-lessons-from-sxsws-mar.php

Lenhart, A., Arafeh, S., Smith, A., & Macgill, A. (2008, April 24). *Writing, Technology and Teens.* Retrieved April 4, 2009, from Pew Internet: http:// www.pewinternet.org/~/media//Files/Reports/2008/ PIP_Writing_Report_FINAL3.pdf.pdf

Lord, R. (2008, February 12). *Beating the ad-avoidance radar.* Retrieved April 6, 2009, from Media Online: http://www.themediaonline.co.za/themedia/view/ themedia/en/page7330?oid=2871&sn=Detail

Lowrey, T. M., Shrum, L. J., & McCarty, J. A. (2005). *The Future of Television Advertising.* Retrieved April 6, 2009, from Dr. L. J. Shrum page at College of Business in The University of Texas at San Antonio: http://faculty.business.utsa.edu/ljshrum/KimmelChapter.PageProofs.pdf

Macklin, B. (2008, April). *Broadband Services: VoIP and IPTV Trends.* Retrieved April 7, 2009, from emarketer: http://www.emarketer.com/Reports/All/Emarketer_2000393.aspx

Macleod, H. (2008, August 1). *the cloud's best-kept secret.* Retrieved April 6, 2009, from gapinvoid: http://www.gapingvoid.com/Moveable_Type/archives/004638.html

Madden, M. (2007, July 25). *Online Videos Go Mainstream.* Retrieved April 7, 2009, from PewResearchCenter Publications: http://pewresearch.org/pubs/552/online-videos-go-mainstream

Majchrzak, A. (2007, April 12). *The Promise of Passion of Collective Wisdom ...through Wikis & the Wiki Way .* Retrieved April 6, 2009, from InThinking Network: http://www.in2in.org/forums/2007/2007%20-%20Conference%20Presentations/Majchrzak%20-%20The%20Passion%20of%20Collective%20Wisdom%20-%20Final.pdf

McAdams, M. (1999, May). *Changing Media, Changing Us.* Retrieved April 2006, 2009, from Cybermedia: http://mindymcadams.com/cybermedia/meyrowitz.html

Meiners, J. (2008, March 19). *General Motors to Spend $1.5 Billion on Online Advertising.* Retrieved April 6, 2009, from Marketing Pilgrim: http://www.marketingpilgrim.com/2008/03/general-motors-to-spend-15-billion-on-online-advertising.html

Meyrowitz, J. (1986). No Sense of Place: the impact of electronic media on social behavior. In J. Meyrowitz, *No Sense of Place.* Oxford University Press US.

Microsoft. (2009, April). *Europe Logs On.* Retrieved April 10, 2009, from Scribd: http://www.scribd.com/doc/14065700/Europe-Logs-On

MillwardBrown. (2007, February). *Lifestyles of the Ad Averse.* Retrieved April 6, 2009, from Microsoft Advertising: http://advertising.microsoft.com/france/WWDocs/User/fr-fr/NewsAndEvents/News/Lifestyles%20of%20the%20Ad%20Averse.pdf

MOAH. (2005, March 28). *Dreams of Steam: the History of Steam Power.* Retrieved April 6, 2009, from Museum of American Heritage: http://www.moah.org/exhibits/archives/steam.html

Moloney, D. (2007, September 7). *2007 Financial analyst Meeting Presentation (slide 75).* Retrieved April 6, 2009, from Motorola: http://media.corporate-ir.net/media_files/irol/90/90829/presentations/MOTfinancialanalystmeeting.pdf

MTV, N. M. (2007, August 1). *MTV, Nickelodeon and Microsoft challenges assumption about relationship between kids and Digital.* Retrieved April 14, 2009, from Microsoft Advertising: http://advertising.microsoft.com/uk/digital-youth-relationship

Murdoch, R. (2007, May 7). *Mixed Media*. Retrieved April 7, 2009, from Forbes: http://www.forbes.com/forbes/2007/0507/138.html

Murphy, P. (2008, July 15). *Do problems with Wikipedia presage social networking's end?* Retrieved April 6, 2009, from ZDNet: http://blogs.zdnet.com/Murphy/?p=1190

Myers, J. (2008, October 21). *TV Industry Faces Ad Avoidance Crisis More Severe Than Financial Crisis, Warns TiVo CEO*. Retrieved April 6, 2009, from The Huffington Post: http://www.huffingtonpost.com/jack-myers/tv-industry-faces-ad-avoi_b_136421.html

Nauert, R. (2008, January 14). *Culture Affects The Way We Use Our Brain*. Retrieved April 5, 2009, from PsychCentral: http://psychcentral.com/news/2008/01/11/culture-affects-the-way-we-use-our-brain/1773.html

NDS. (2007, April). *The Death of Primetime?* Retrieved April 6, 2009, from NDS: http://www.nds.com/pdfs/DeathofPrimetime_TVAsia_Apr07.pdf

North, D. C. (2005). *Understanding the Process of Economic Change*. Princeton University Press.

O'Leary, N. (2008, Nov 17). *Welcome to My World - It's the consumer's media universe -- you just market in it*. Retrieved April 7, 2009, from AdWeek: http://www.adweek.com/aw/content_display/news/agency/e3i7a86dc0b860b7b35bf57e85a3e094cfe?pn=1

Ong, W. J. (1988). *Orality and Literacy: The Technologizing of the Word*. Routledge.

Ong, W. J. (1971). *Rhetoric, Romance, and Technology*. Cornell University Press.

O'Sullivan, J. (2000, April 3). *CAMPAIGN 2000 III: Our Inglorious Revolution - race and culture in 2000 presidential campaign - Brief Article*. Retrieved April 4, 2009, from BNET Business Network: http://findarticles.com/p/articles/mi_m1282/is_6_52/ai_60137469/

Owyang, J. (2008, March 12). *A Groundswell at SXSW: How The Audience Revolted and Asserted Control* . Retrieved April 7, 2009, from Web Strategy by Jeremiah: http://www.web-strategist.com/blog/2008/03/12/a-groundswell-at-sxsw-how-the-audience-revolted-and-asserted-control/

Parrack, D. (2007, November 4). *Is PC era coming to an end? - New gadgets stealing their market*. Retrieved April 7, 2009, from Tech.Blorge: http://tech.blorge.com/Structure:%20/2007/11/04/is-pc-era-coming-to-an-end-new-gadgets-stealing-their-market/

Pletz, J. (2004, May 3). *Dell changed industry with direct sales*. Retrieved April 7, 2009, from statesman.com: http://www.statesman.com/business/content/business/stories/archive/0503dell.html

Postrel, V. (2005, June). *Consumer Vertigo - A new wave of social critics claim that freedom's just another word for way too much to choose. Here's why they're wrong*. Retrieved April 7, 2009, from Reason online: http://www.reason.com/news/show/36172.html

Prange, D. (2008, March 28). *Pingg and the Evolution of Language*. Retrieved April 5, 2009, from Strategic Name Development: http://www.namedevelopment.com/blog/archives/2008/03/pingg_and_the_e_1.html

Prensky, M. (2001, October). *Digital Natives, Digital Immigrants*. Retrieved April 5, 2009, from marcprensky.com: http://www.marcprensky.com/writing/Prensky%20-%20Digital%20Natives,%20Digital%20Immigrants%20-%20Part1.pdf

Rajaraman, A. (2008, july 9). *The Real Long Tail: Why both Chris Anderson and Anita Elberse are Wrong*. Retrieved April 6, 2009, from Datawocky: http://anand.typepad.com/datawocky/2008/07/the-real-long-tail-why-both-chris-anderson-and-anita-elberse-are-wrong.html

Reed, L. W. (2006, June). *Seven Principles of Sound Public Policy*. Retrieved April 6, 2009, from Mackinac Center for Public Policy: http://www.mackinac.org/article.aspx?ID=3832

RIAA. (2007). *2007 Consumer Profile*. Retrieved April 7, 2009, from Recording Industry Association of America: http://76.74.24.142/44510E63-7B5E-5F42-DA74-349B51EDCE0F.pdf

Rorty, R. (2007, June 11). *Democracy and philosophy*. Retrieved April 6, 2009, from Eurozine: http://www.eurozine.com/articles/2007-06-11-rorty-en.html

Rosvall, M. (2003, February 3). *Complex Networks and Dynamics of an Information Network Model*. Retrieved April 6, 2009, from Theoretical Physics, Umeå University, Sweden: http://www.tp.umu.se/~rosvall/papers/rosvall_masterthesis_03-02-06.pdf

Saint Louis University. (2008). *the life and scholarship of Walter J. Ong, SJ*. Retrieved April 5, 2009, from Saint Louis University: http://www.slu.edu/colleges/AS/ENG/ong/influence.html

Sanders, A. (n.d.). *manuscript to print*. Retrieved April 6, 2009, from English 211 - Goucher College: http://faculty.goucher.edu/eng211/manuscript_to_print.htm

Schmidt, A. (2007, November 7). *Privacy is not an option*. Retrieved April 6, 2009, from Walking Paper: http://www.walkingpaper.org/513

Schwartz, B. (2005, July). *Paradox of Choice presentation*. Retrieved April 7, 2009, from TED Ideas worth spreading: http://www.ted.com/index.php/speakers/barry_schwartz.html

Schwartz, B. (2006, April 27). *The Paradox of Choice - Why more is Less: Presentation at Google*. Retrieved April 7, 2009, from Google Video: http://video.google.com/videoplay?docid=6127548813950043200

Schwartz, B. (2004, April). *The Tyranny of Choice*. Retrieved April 7, 2009, from Prof. Barry Schwartz page at Swarthmore: http://www.swarthmore.edu/SocSci/bschwar1/Sci.Amer.pdf

Sheen, D. (n.d.). *The Boiling Frog*. Retrieved April 5, 2009, from davidsheen.com: http://www.davidsheen.com/b/b2.htm

Shirky, C. (2003, February 10). *Power Laws, Weblogs, and Inequality*. Retrieved April 6, 2009, from Clay Shriky's Writings About the Internet: http://www.shirky.com/writings/powerlaw_weblog.html

Siderman, R. (2007, October 10). *Cable vs. Telco: The Battle Heats Up.* Retrieved April 6, 2009, from BusinessWeek: http://www.businessweek.com/investor/content/oct2007/pi20071010_242433.htm

Skrenta, R. (2007, January 1). *Winner-Take-All: Google and the Third Age of Computing.* Retrieved April 6, 2009, from Skrentablog: http://www.skrenta.com/2007/01/winnertakeall_google_and_the_t.html

Sloan, R., & Thompson, M. (2005, January). *Epic 2015.* Retrieved April 7, 2009, from Albino Blacksheep: http://www.albinoblacksheep.com/flash/epic

Solis, B. (2008, March 10). *Sarah Lacy on Sarah Lacy and the SXSW Mark Zuckerberg Keynote.* Retrieved April 7, 2009, from PR 2.0: http://www.briansolis.com/2008/03/sarah-lacy-on-sarah-lacy-and-sxsw-mark.html

Spitznagel, C. R. (2000). *Graph Theory and the Bridges of Königsberg .* Retrieved April 6, 2009, from John Carrel University: http://www.jcu.edu/math/vignettes/bridges.htm

Stuart, G. (2008, September 8). *You Can't Avoid Ad Avoidance.* Retrieved April 6, 2009, from Ad Week: https://secure.vnuemedia.com/aw/content_display/community/columns/other-columns/e3id9a975e26c8545c5a020bb0908182476

Stuart, G., & Vizu. (2008, September). *Why Consumers Hate Advertising & What They Are Doing About It.* Retrieved April 6, 2009, from Vizu: http://answers.vizu.com/solutions/pr/pdf/Why_Consumers_Hate_Ads.pdf

Swanwick, T. (2008, January 28). It's a Badge of Honor. *Courier Mail .* Brisbane, Australia.

Swartz, A. (2006, September 4). *Who Writes Wikipedia?* Retrieved 4 6, 2009, from Raw Thought: http://www.aaronsw.com/weblog/whowriteswikipedia

Tabuchi, H. (2007, November 4). *PCs losing their relevance in Japan.* Retrieved April 7, 2009, from USA Today: http://www.usatoday.com/tech/products/2007-11-04-822783149_x.htm

Telecompetitor. (2007, Aug 2). *Comcast Overtakes Vonage.* Retrieved April 6, 2009, from telecompetitor: http://telecompetitor.com/node/249

Thompson, C. (2008, September 5). *Brave New World of Digital Intimacy.* Retrieved April 6, 2009, from The New York Times: http://www.nytimes.com/2008/09/07/magazine/07awareness-t.html?_r=2

Thys, A. (2009, April 9). *Will the Internet Overtake Television in 2010?* Retrieved April 10, 2009, from FutureLab: http://blog.futurelab.net/2009/04/will_the_internet_overtake_tel.html

Varga, G. (2006, April 9). *Vanishing act.* Retrieved April 7, 2009, from SignOnSanDiego.com: http://www.signonsandiego.com/news/features/20060409-9999-1a09albums.html

Varian, H., Hall, J., Jain, M., Lee, S., Pechon, A., Skucha, K., et al. (2007, March 20). *Future Labor Markets - Technology Assessment.* Retrieved April 6, 2009, from UC Berkeley School of Information: http://people.ischool.berkeley.edu/~hal/Courses/StratTech07/Tech/Preso/F-labor-paper.pdf

Vedrashko, I. (2007, November 6). *Automatic Ad Skiping In 1934.* Retrieved April 6, 2009, from Ad Lab: http://adverlab.blogspot.com/2007/11/automatic-ad-skipping-in-1934.html

Vedrashko, I. (2007, September 10). *Study: Banners Work Even when Overlooked.* Retrieved April 6, 2009, from Ad Lab: http://adverlab.blogspot.com/2007/09/study-banners-work-even-when-overlooked.html

Veenhoven, R. (2005). *Happiness in multiple-choice society.* Retrieved April 7, 2009, from Prof. Ruut Veenhoven page at Erasmus Universiteit Rotterdam : http://www2.eur.nl/fsw/research/veenhoven/Pub2000s/2005n.htm

Wallace, L. (2008, March 11). *SXSW: 2008, the Year the Audience Keynoted.* Retrieved April 7, 2009, from Wired: http://blog.wired.com/underwire/2008/03/sxsw-2008-the-y.html

Wallis, C. (2006, March 19). *The Multitasking Generation.* Retrieved April 4, 2009, from Time U.S.: http://www.time.com/time/magazine/article/0,9171,1174696,00.html

Wang, S., Mukherjee, S., & Anninger, S. (2007, June). *Entertainment Industry; A longer Look at the Long Tail.* Retrieved April 7, 2009, from Bear Stearns: http://www.bearstearns.com/bservlet/BSFile?filePath=I60QwqJMFL0MFhHqI8HkYegbHVSVCr%2BWe4EAYKWikL5LWp6KzJC2Sg%3D%3D&preview=yes

Warmington and Rose. (1999). *Great Dialogues of Plato: Complete Texts of the Republic, Apology, Crito Phaido, Ion, and Meno, vol.1.* New York: Warmington and Rose.

Wikipedia. (2009, February 23). *Orality.* Retrieved April 5, 2009, from Wikipedia: http://en.wikipedia.org/wiki/Orality

Yahoo_Answers. (2008). *What is the point of instant messaging?* Retrieved April 5, 2009, from Yahoo Answers: http://answers.yahoo.com/question/index?qid=20080606105449AAsGGrp

Zanini, M. (2008, November). *Using 'power curves' to assess industry dynamics .* Retrieved April 6, 2009, from The McKinsey Quarterly: http://www.mckinseyquarterly.com/Strategy/Growth/Using_power_curves_to_assess_industry_dynamics_2222

About the Author

Orestes is passionate about helping business teams to better understand their consumers and market trends, identifying opportunities to grow business value and to improve people's lives.

Orestes has accumulated a broad experience dealing with diverse consumers and markets, working as a marketing and strategy executive at Eastman Kodak, Johnson & Johnson and his own company (a software developer and automation services provider), where he faced diverse strategic challenges in many different product categories in different countries, regions and at global level.

Orestes' focus on consumers coupled with strong analytical skills and fact-based leadership were instrumental in building his proven track record of above-goal results and successful turnarounds. He has led business' teams on identifying and leveraging market opportunities to reverse profitability and market share declines, to reinforce brands and to launch new products, new promotions and campaigns.

Orestes holds an electronic engineering degree from Instituto Tecnologico de Aeronautica (ITA) and a Masters degree (MBA) from Fundacao Getulio Vargas (FGV).

Originally from Brazil, Orestes is fluent in English, Spanish and Portuguese. He currently lives in Rochester, New York, with his wife and two sons.